I – Operations:

How the Internet can transform your Operating Model

Published by
Indaba Publishing
Woodside, California
Telephone: 1(866) 9-INDABA
www.indabapublishing.com

ISBN 0-9678541-2-1

10 9 8 7 6 5 4 3 2 1

Printed in Canada
Previously published by The Institute Press, Inc.

I – Operations:
How the Internet can transform your Operating Model

by

Gary Daichendt and Brett Johnson

Published by Indaba Publishing

www.iOperations.com

Contact information:

Brett Johnson
brett@iOperations.com
www.inst.net

Gary Daichendt
gary@iOperations.com

Why we co-authored this book

The purpose of this book is to convey the characteristics of successful companies in the Internet Economy and the common experiences leading to their success.

Internet-enabled operations (I-Operations) is the emerging Operating Model of the New Economy. Our intention is to share a recipe for the successful creation and implementation of this model.

Two criteria are of utmost importance in assembling and imparting the information on I-Operations. The first is credibility. Brett Johnson, founder and President of The Institute, contributes objectivity independent of Cisco, and experience in correctly interpreting research results. He has justifiably earned a reputation for performing objective analysis with integrity. The second criterion is to add value to businesses in search of success in the Internet Economy. Brett's experience in leveraging all aspects of the operating model to increase corporate impact significantly heightened the probability that we would achieve this goal. Brett has had the opportunity to observe the operations of Cisco, several of Cisco's competitors, and many participants from other industries.

Hopefully, the combination of our past and present business experiences, the statistically representative research, and the analytical approach to interpretation have produced the validity and value we seek.

Gary Daichendt

Every day new Internet-related technologies challenge the experience and thinking of senior executives. Traditional notions of what it takes to create impact are outdated, and executives need fresh frameworks for evaluating and applying emerging technologies to their corporations. The Internet has dramatically affected the requirements for winning in your particular sphere, whether business, non-profit or government. Few corporations have mastered the art of designing and implementing an end-to-end Operating Model that forcefully supports its core purpose. Fewer still have discovered how an Internet-enabled Operating Model can transform their business. Cisco has been recognized as a company that has. Our research uncovered others who have made substantial progress, and this book is our attempt to share the principles that have brought them success.

Some of the executives we interviewed at more traditional companies argued that Cisco may not be a great example of a company that has implemented an Internet-enabled Operating Model, since they have always been Internet-savvy. I therefore considered it a double-coup to be able to work with Gary Daichendt. His career spans the worlds of Old Economy and New Economy companies. As former Executive Vice President of Worldwide Operations at Cisco, Gary is in a unique position to offer insights on Cisco's operations, as well as commentary on how other businesses have implemented Internet-enabled Operating Models. Executives who span the range from Dot-com to traditional corporations will find his thoughts direct and refreshing.

Brett Johnson

Preface

The first edition of *I-Operations* was written at the tail end of the Dot-com boom. With the economy having won the battle over the excesses of that short phase of Internet history, it is tempting to blank the boom from our corporate memory. Not so fast. The I-Operations book has always made an intentional distinction between the Internet Economy and the flurry of Dot-com activities that climaxed in 2000. The principles espoused in I-Operations are applicable to corporations in all industries and in all stages of development. While the names of Dot-com companies become quickly dated, the lessons they teach us should not be ignored. It would be a mistake to not learn from the positive aspects of the Dot-com era, including the technological innovation, cultural agility, and economic experimentation. We should also learn from the failure to consider the entire Operating Model—end-to-end—from the outset. And it is this tenet that I-Operations addresses.

Our primary audience remains the executive in an organization that was founded on brick and mortar. They may be the ones to most reap the benefits of the Internet Economy as they have the disciplines and management depth to execute I-Operations, whereas their Dot-com predecessors had ideas that they could not sustain.

Someone recently contended with us that the Internet is old technology without having read our broad definition. Obviously technology has changed radically since the first edition. This book is not about the latest technology. It remains a CxO handbook on how to think about and act upon emerging technologies that are cultural and corporate change agents across organizations and societies. Many of these are related in some way to the Internet. Before digging into I-Operations, please take a moment to read some key definitions. Grasp these, and you will have the essence of I-Operations.

Defining I-Operations

A set of working definitions will provide some handles for the discussion that follows in the rest of this book. Additional terms are contained in the glossary.

- A **Physical Enterprise** is a business or organization comprised of people and assets with a common objective.
- A **Virtual Enterprise** is an organizing principle for internal and external entities who share in information access, decision-making and value creation activities.
- **Internet:** the technologies and deployment of all internets, intranets, extranets and the World Wide Web for all types of information, including voice, video, data and image.
- A **New World Application** is an application that ostensibly utilizes the Internet to significantly improve the profitability or market share of a company.
- **Internet-enabled** is the use of New World Applications in a Virtual Enterprise.
- The **Operating Model** of an organization is the processes and procedures it uses to design, build, market, and manage its products and services.
- **Operations:** The execution of the Operating Model.
- **I-Operations:** Internet-enabled operations.

A company has I-Operations when they have deployed New World Applications in the context of a Virtual Enterprise to execute their Operating Model.

There is no debate that the Internet is a major factor in society and business. In fact, the Internet Economy is the economic context in which business is conducted today. The first section of this book traces the history and dynamics of the Internet that make it a force to be embraced.

There have been many misconceptions about Internet-based business, and there are also assumptions from historical business practice that do not apply to this New Economy. In the second section of *I-Operations*, we lay out eight challenges to those wanting to participate in the Internet Economy.

These challenges mandate a new approach. In this third section, we begin to share the findings of our research and suggest key definitions and practical frameworks for achieving I-Operations. We expand on a simple action statement, "Get the right people doing the right things within the right framework."

The fourth section paints a picture of the results of I-Operations for a variety of corporations, including traditional businesses, Dot-coms, companies that were "born wired", and social sector organizations.

More than ever, corporations need a business philosophy that leads to sustained results. Having seen many seven-day wonders in the Internet arena, this section examines how implementing I-Operations enables corporations to achieve sustainable impact in the Internet Economy.

Prior to our conclusions on I-Operations, we share personal perspectives on the type of leadership that the Internet demands, particularly given the increased visibility of, and rapid market response to, the pluses and minuses of leaders. In the final chapter we pull the many facets together to encourage readers as they pursue their particular opportunities in the Internet Economy.

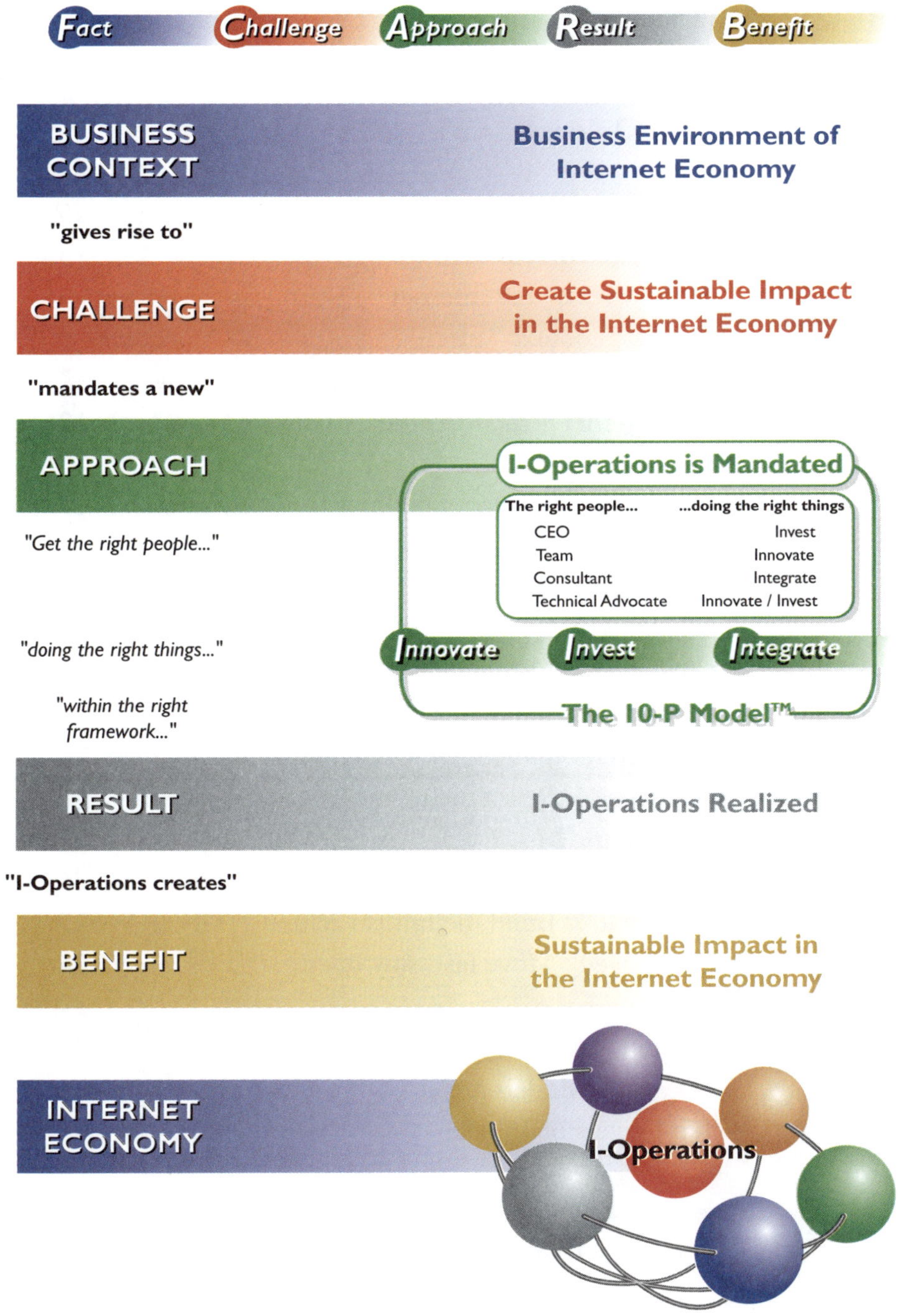
Fact
Challenge
Approach
Result
Benefit
BUSINESS CONTEXT
Business Environment of Internet Economy
"gives rise to"
CHALLENGE
Create Sustainable Impact in the Internet Economy
"mandates a new"
APPROACH
I-Operations is Mandated
The right people...
...doing the right things
CEO
Invest
Team
Innovate
Consultant
Integrate
Technical Advocate
Innovate / Invest
"Get the right people..."
"doing the right things..."
"within the right framework..."
Innovate
Invest
Integrate
The 10-P Model™
RESULT
I-Operations Realized
"I-Operations creates"
BENEFIT
Sustainable Impact in the Internet Economy
INTERNET ECONOMY
I-Operations

Table of Contents

Is This Book for You?

This book's intended reader is the executive who desires his or her business to participate to the fullest extent in the New Economy, the Internet Economy. Whether you are representing a long established corporation, an emerging enterprise, or a newly formed business operating on Internet time, it is our desire that you gain insightful direction for your company's success.

Detailed statistical research on successful companies in the Internet Economy is a distinguishing characteristic of this book. We draw upon the success of the current leaders for inspiration to those of you not yet participating, and propose specific actions to enable your success.

We expect this book to be a dynamic document as we are truly in the early stages of the Internet Economy. The fluctuating fortunes of the technology sector in no way negate the need for I-Operations; in our view, an end-to-end renewal of Operating Models is essential, regardless of market conditions. The continual change in core technologies makes this perpetual renewal a must for all organizations.

A Frenchman recently asked a Chinese gentleman what he thought of the French Revolution. "It's too soon to tell," came the reply. Perhaps it is too soon to tell what the impacts of the Internet Revolution are for your corporation, but we believe it's not too early or too late to develop a framework for asking the right questions.

If you are asking questions, this book is for you.

Chapter 1

I-Operations

Executive Overview

The Internet Revolution is upon us. The impact of this technological revolution on people, businesses, and societies has been compared many times to that of the Industrial Revolution. The effects of this latest revolution are profound and will continue to be so. Of course, there will be other future technological revolutions that will leave their mark on future societies. In September 1999, 92% of CEOs worldwide believed the Internet would have a major impact on the global marketplace within three years.[1] It is our assumption that you have already concluded that the impact is dramatic for you, your business, and perhaps your country. (Our definition of business is broad and includes any corporation engaged in for profit, non-profit, academic, government, and social sector endeavors.)

Beginning with the premise that the Internet Economy is a fact of business, we have focused specifically on the company characteristics that are successful in the Internet Economy, and prescribed the actions necessary to ensure that these characteristics are part of your organization's culture and Operating Model. We refer to this group of characteristics as I-Operations, or Internet-enabled operations. The recipe for success is available to anyone who is prepared to change.

We have found that companies that are already successful participants in this Internet Economy have three compelling attributes:

1. They recognize the Internet phenomenon and its potential impact on their organization and their industry.

2. They have successfully deployed a New World Application using the power of the Internet to contribute significantly to their bottom line profitability, market share, or both.

3. They have agile corporate cultures. Even though human beings naturally resist change, successful companies have set up an organizational culture that accepts change as inevitable, and embraces it.

Over 80% of our study participants indicated they recognize the Internet phenomenon and its potential impact on them.[2] A much smaller percentage of participants have the remaining two attributes. The recipe for developing all three attributes is not complex, but does require a proper framework and careful execution of I-Operations.

Through the study results, focus group executive interviews, and thousands of client meetings, we found that three common actions have been taken to incubate and implement New World Applications and to stimulate corporate cultures.

A. Get the right people…

- The CEO to create the environment.
- A cross-functional team of experts to incubate and implement the application.

- A consultant external to your organization or company to implement the application along with the appropriate internal people resources.
- A senior level technical advocate to evangelize the use of the Internet.

B. Doing the right things…

- Innovate
- Invest
- Integrate

C. Within the right framework.

- An end-to-end look at the Operating Model. (For our purposes we are using The Institute's 10-P Model™.)

What these action statements say is just as important as what they do not say. For example, they do not say that the CEO or the CIO will be the originator of your New World Application. In fact, overwhelming odds state they will not.

Participation in the Internet Revolution is no more an option than was participation in the Industrial Revolution. Use of the Internet will be as pervasive as other technological innovations such as the railroad, automobile, telephone, and microprocessor. The Internet will not eradicate all of your business issues. However, with hundreds of billions of dollars of infrastructure that encompasses virtually all countries, a forecasted user population of 1 billion in the year 2005, and e-commerce estimates in the trillions of dollars, it is not a force to be ignored![3]

It is our hope that our research of today's I-Operations will provide insights to assist with your success tomorrow.

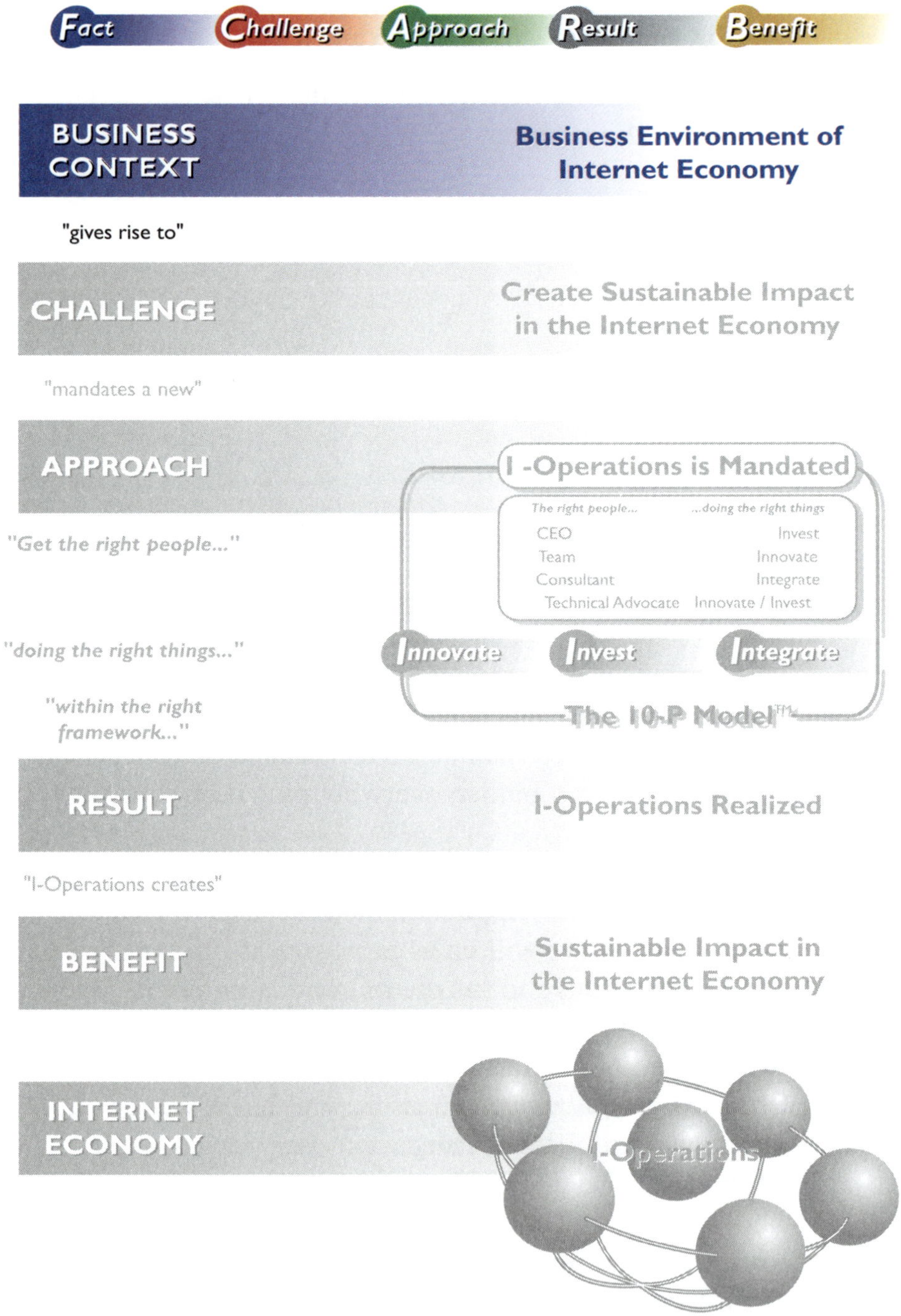
Fact
Challenge
Approach
Result
Benefit
BUSINESS CONTEXT
Business Environment of Internet Economy
"gives rise to"
CHALLENGE
Create Sustainable Impact in the Internet Economy
"mandates a new"
APPROACH
I -Operations is Mandated
The right people...
...doing the right things
CEO
Invest
Team
Innovate
Consultant
Integrate
Technical Advocate
Innovate / Invest
"Get the right people..."
"doing the right things..."
"within the right framework..."
Innovate
Invest
Integrate
The 10-P Model™
RESULT
I-Operations Realized
"I-Operations creates"
BENEFIT
Sustainable Impact in the Internet Economy
INTERNET ECONOMY
I-Operations

Chapter 2

Fact

The Business Environment in the Internet Economy

There is no denying that the Internet has already created massive changes in communication, business and society at large. There is also much agreement on the fact that we are still in the early stages of this revolution. With the rapid rate of change associated with Internet technologies, it is important to step back from the current state of the Internet and gain a sense of its context before we examine our case for I-Operations.

Historical context

Technology has had a profound effect on the course of history, but it has seldom been the sole driver of change. There are often a number of converging trends at work that result in fundamental change in society. Sometimes this convergence of trends has a disruptive effect and causes new paradigms to emerge. This disruption can be socio-political, socio-economic or of some other nature.

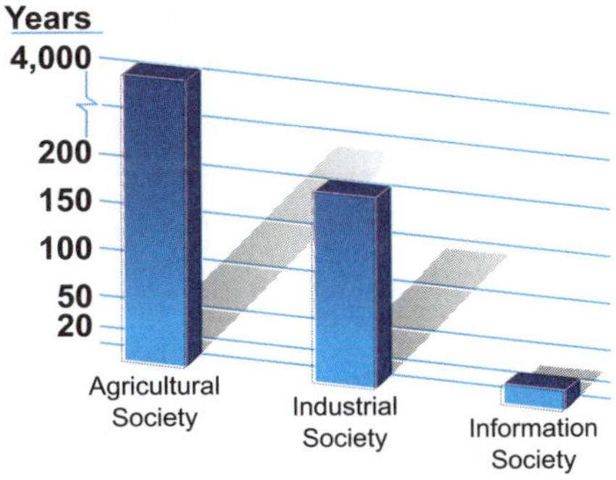

The shift from a hunter-gatherer society to an

agricultural one came about as a result of a change in the Operating Model of food production. The agricultural revolution involved a cultural shift, as well as a technological shift. The new technology was the ability to increase production of food using fields and farming. The cultural shift was that people became less nomadic, because they no longer had to rely on hunting and gathering to supply their food. Furthermore, fewer workers were needed to ensure the food supply, freeing more people to pursue other non-agricultural activities. In essence, there was a productivity gain that resulted from the convergence of cultural and technological change.

Movable type, invented by Johannes Gutenberg in the 1450s was a prime technology driver of the Reformation and Renaissance movements of the 15th and 16th Centuries. These movements fostered a new cultural environment, which led to innovation in science, business and the political systems of the day.

The Industrial Age of the 18th and 19th Centuries is perhaps the greatest example in history of the impact of technology on the course of economic and social change. Key inventions such as the steam engine fueled the Industrial Revolution and changed the face of business and society forever.

The Information Age followed the Industrial Age with its breakthrough technology, the transistor. With follow-on technologies, such as the microprocessor, the Information Age initiated the shift from mechanical automation to information processing. The primary thrust of the early decades of the Information Age was the automation of routine processes and calculations. The incredible cycle of increasing computer power and decreasing costs created tremendous opportunities for corporations to deploy information technology throughout their organization.

Then came the Internet, ushering in a time of unprecedented change. The Internet has opened the information floodgates and enabled innovation as never before. A key differentiator that the Internet brings is information access from anywhere by anyone. As low bandwidth voice and data capabilities give way to Converged Communications—the integration of voice, video and data on a single IP network—the economic and social impact continues its revolutionary pattern. The business winners in this new age will be those who adapt to this change and develop Operating Models that can take advantage of the new opportunities presented by network and Internet technologies.

Integrated Converged Applications. Applications that have a holistic or integrated view of how the end user uses information, seeking to deliver such information and functionality across a spectrum of delivery mechanisms (such as PDA, cell phone, pocket computer, mobile IP phone, IP phone, and Web browser) in as seamless a manner as possible.

Technology has clearly been a factor in most major social and economic changes throughout history. Technology that radically increased communication and productivity has had the greatest impact, and has been a disruptive force to traditional Operating Models.

Four waves of the Internet

First Wave: Brochure-ware

In the early days of the Internet, organizations viewed it primarily as a marketing tool. The Internet held the prospect of thousands, if not millions, of users. Companies saw value in promoting themselves with a website. The major function of the site was as an online marketing brochure and, at most, an online catalogue.

Second Wave: Business to Customer e-Commerce

As the number of Internet users increased, it was not difficult for companies to see the potential for generating a vast customer base from the online population. E-commerce technology was developed and deployed in the second wave to extend the functionality of the brochure-ware sites and provide order placement and payment capabilities. It was in this wave of the Internet that we witnessed the explosive growth in Dot-com businesses as the e-commerce business model became viable. With the emergence of this business model the barriers to entry were lowered. Now any Dot-com company could have a global market reach without all of the startup costs of a traditional company. The Web became a fertile ground for business, and the e-commerce business model became the darling of Wall Street, seemingly overnight.

Third Wave: Business-to-Business

The logical next step in the evolution of the Internet business model is the Business-to-Business (B2B) model. Forecasters expect B2B transactions over the Internet to grow from $131 billion in 1999 to $1.5 trillion in 2003[4]. Internet-enabled Electronic Data Interchange (EDI) will account for a large number of these transactions as businesses adopt technologies that allow them to synchronize their EDI capabilities with partners through the Internet.

Fourth Wave: e-Everywhere

The e-everywhere phase is that stage where the technology itself is ubiquitous and almost transparent. Web-enabled applications become the norm and people are highly accessible via the Internet and other communications media. Boundaries are eliminated between stakeholders—those people inside and outside your organization who have a stake in its success, including customers, investors, employees and suppliers. Intelligent agents could initiate and sustain communication between appliances with no human intervention. For example, a computer system could monitor the power load levels of a power grid. If a brownout were imminent, it would communicate over the Internet to home and industry appliances in the area, adjusting thermostats and shutting off discretionary devices. The brownout is avoided, the utility's clients are more satisfied, and the utility's production facilities are utilized more effectively, thus saving money. Ideally, the consumer would participate voluntarily and also receive financial incentives in our futuristic, but not unrealistic, example. With e-everywhere, the Network has the intelligence to translate the message into the right media—voice, video or text—for the chosen appliance (computer, PDA, phone, pager, etc.).

Business context

The business environment in the Internet Economy is exemplified by significant worker productivity increases. Through new uses of technology, particularly communication infrastructures, companies enter new markets or gain competitive advantage. The United States has enjoyed worker productivity increases of 4.4% since 1995. U.S. Department of Commerce research[5] indicates that this is due in large measure to technology improvements, and their extended use by the American worker. In fact, the U.S. has had its longest period of economic prosperity, with relatively low inflation, thanks to these productivity gains.

Virtual Close. The ability to close the books at any time. First pioneered by Cisco, and now a hallmark of companies that have the process efficiencies and agility associated with the Internet Economy.

Virtual Manufacturing. The ability to manufacture products outside of a corporation's own boundaries and in a manner that is transparent to customers.

Businesses and organizations benefit the most from these impressive productivity results. Cisco Systems' average revenue productivity per employee in December 2000 was

$710,000[6]. Admittedly, Cisco is in a high productivity market segment. However, Cisco reached this productivity with an employee population of over 38,000[6] through the extensive use of New World Applications. Examples of New World Applications deployed at Cisco include: virtual manufacturing, virtual close, online client support, e-commerce, e-learning and employee empowerment, to name a few.

Brick and Mortar. A traditional organization whose assets and service delivery mechanisms are primarily physical.

The uses of these technologies have their quintessential representation in the Internet. The Internet includes the incorporation of data, voice, and video on intranets, extranets, internets and the World Wide Web. New markets have been created and entered, such as online retail shopping, branchless banking, electronic brokerage, online auctions, and B2B exchanges. To be fair, some of these new entrants have appeared, and then disappeared, in a relatively short period of time. Established businesses, often referred to as brick and mortar companies, have seen their assets turned to liabilities and their market models threatened.

As an example, over 60% of automobile buyers in the U.S. now check the Internet first prior to physically visiting a traditional dealership. This immediately results in a more informed consumer. Distribution models have to adjust to this significant (and rapidly growing) statistic. The long-term result will be a fundamental shift in the Operating Model of how automobiles are designed, developed, marketed and delivered to the consumer. Automobile dealerships, automobile manufacturers, or new distribution entities can capture or lose the prize of consumer recognition and trust for their brand names. Being in the business longer is not necessarily the advantage it used to be. In fact, progress in the Internet Economy for a tenured brick and mortar enterprise is usually inhibited in two ways. The internal culture is adverse to change, and the past methods (or mistakes) can be used against the established business by a new entrant's image and marketing. This is not to say that businesses with established longevity and assets lose their advantages. However, existing culture and business practices can seriously hinder the success of the established business enterprise in the Internet Economy.

AutoNation is a publicly traded corporation that serves around 400 automobile dealerships across the U.S. It has attained impressive results in this market-segment. Its Internet-related sales were over $1.8 billion in 2001 ($1 billion in 1999).[7] "Using the Internet as a sales medium represents the biggest fundamental change in automobile distribution in 100 years," says Michael Jackson, AutoNation's Chief Executive Officer. Automobile purchases can be investigated and consummated online via AutoNation's website at www.AutoNation.com. Multiple makes and styles of autos are available. Insurance, financing, and delivery can be arranged using keystrokes in the comfort of your living room 24 hours a day, 7 days a week. The user interface, information service and buying experience is synonymous with the AutoNation brand.

A New World Application is by definition one that has significant positive effect on the bottom line or market share of a business. These applications are based on the use of communication infrastructures, both external and internal to a business. Businesses in rapidly changing market-segments are in a time-critical, competitive race to deploy these applications to their advantage. This race is fueled by the proliferation of the Internet, and the ample funding available in up-markets. Venture Capitalists alone placed $54 billion in start-up funding in the first half of 2000.[8] It was never easier to go into business in the history of business! What we predicted in the first edition of *I-Operations* has been proven true: It has also never been easier to go out of business! During down-markets, the pressure to cut costs weeds out frivolous applications and fuels a demand for efficiency-oriented deployments of technology.

The Internet and its impact on today's business operations is hard to ignore. Some may point to the rash of Dotcom failures as a sign that business on the Internet is just a fad. However, evidence suggests that most start-ups have failed due to poor management, not poor concepts. Poor management manifests itself in many ways, such as inadequate economic models (assuming, for example, that advertising revenues will increase continuously) and failure to create barriers to entry.

The time to embrace the Internet and its all-encompassing Internet Economy is now. The way to do so is by empowering your organization with I-Operations.

This is your business in the Internet Economy

> In the Internet Age it is not the technology that creates new wealth, but radical new business concepts. So every company that was "built to last," must now be "rebuilt to change."[9]

We go beyond this statement to say that every corporation needs to do what it takes to have sustainable impact. Impact goes beyond change. Much of the froth in the Internet market was due to a philosophy of change and trying to be different for the sake of being different. To endure, you have to have a core business that creates impact. The Internet is one of those enabling technologies that allows you to radically redefine how to create sustained impact.

The Internet is fueling massive cultural change

We believe that large-scale cultural change takes place when three catalysts are present:

- Trends in politics, economics, society and technology collide.
- An enabling technology feeds or leads the trends.
- The normal rate of change is radically altered by some unforeseen advancement.

The cable network A&E recently ran the program, "Biography of the Millennium: 100 People—1,000 years." They interviewed leaders from all industries. In the end, Johannes Gutenberg was proclaimed to be the most influential person of the last millennium. His invention of the movable-type press in the middle of the fifteenth century changed society forever. The printing press completely changed the way information could be shared and disseminated. Gutenberg's invention fueled some of the most important cultural changes that were to come, including the Reformation, the Enlightenment, and the Industrial Revolution. It also orchestrated the creation of the "middle class" as the free flow of information between common men and women gave power to the people, and struck the fatal blow to the absolute rule of the elite.

Historians affirm that Gutenberg did not create movable type in order to transform society. But his personal passion and technological innovation collided with religious and socio-political trends to begin a phenomenal revolution of ideas and practice. The environment was ripe for cultural change; the enabling technology fed the revolution.

Whether the Internet deserves all the credit or not, we are in the midst of an incredible change. As Rolf Jensen, the renowned futurist and author of *The Dream Society,* has stated:

> The Information Society will render itself obsolete through automation... Soon we will probably see the birth of a new type of society, a new economic foundation for business.[10]

Many agree that we are in the early stages of the Internet's transformation of our society. It is not technology alone that is creating this change. But there is a confluence of factors—of which the Internet is one—that is contributing to the cultural change that is currently underway.

A related observation is that the cultural dynamics are without boundaries; the inter-relationship between culture and other elements of the Operating Model are plainly visible.

The Internet is a fact of life. It is changing the thinking of constituents inside and outside the corporation. It is transforming, if not re-inventing, the context in which business is conducted. The Internet Economy is one of speed, innovation and excitement. It carries promise of high risks and high rewards. Yet it also has the dynamics of past revolutions; it has a mixture of fad and fact. Within this context of the New Economy, we are still left with a challenge: how to create sustainable impact in the Internet Economy.

The Internet Economy is the new context for business

The emergence of the Internet and network technologies has resulted in the creation of new business models, drastically altering more traditional models. Many of the first wave of Internet businesses will not endure the Dot-com shakedown. There will be much consolidation within industries. However, many new Internet-enabled models will emerge to change the face of business. Those companies that embrace change and take advantage of opportunities in the New Economy will ultimately emerge as the leaders.

Questions/Statements to Ponder

Has the emergence of the Internet altered your value proposition?

Are you leveraging the global reach of the Internet to access new markets?

How do I leverage the Internet to communicate my unique story?

Benchmarking the Internet Economy: Years to 50 Million Users

Our century has already witnessed the birth and phenomenal growth of multiple breakthrough technologies which have forever changed our ways of inter-relating. What is striking is that the transition to Internet-based e-business is making all previous examples look like they arrived at a snail's pace.

The chart illustrates the number of years it took for each successive communications technology in this century to build up to a consumer population of 50 million. Time to market has been dropping precipitously even though each development brought with it the need to lay a new infrastructure of appliances and equipment.

Number of Years to Reach 50 Million Users

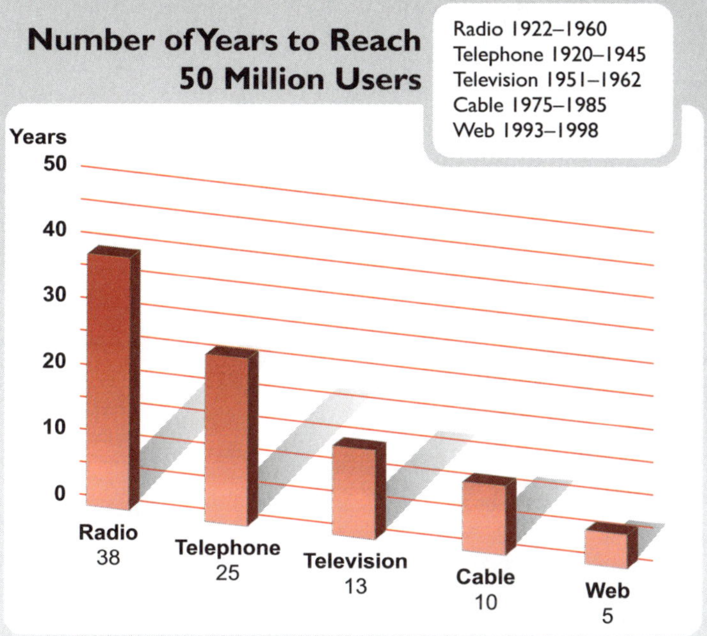

Source: e-business: A Practical Perspective "Turning an Economy Inside Out" page 12 November 17, 1999, The Delphi Group[11]

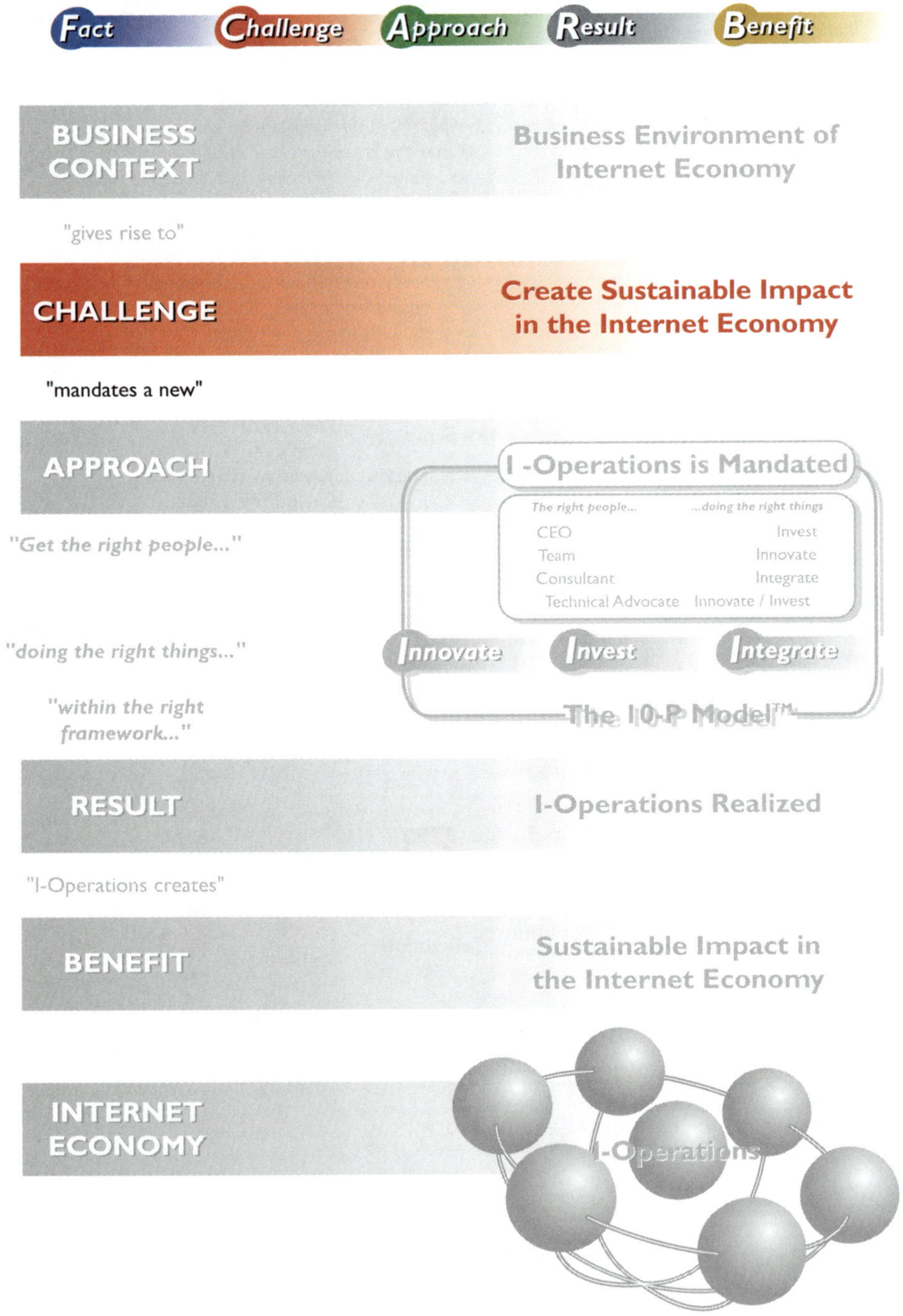
Fact
Challenge
Approach
Result
Benefit
BUSINESS CONTEXT
Business Environment of Internet Economy
"gives rise to"
CHALLENGE
Create Sustainable Impact in the Internet Economy
"mandates a new"
APPROACH
I -Operations is Mandated
The right people...
...doing the right things
CEO
Invest
Team
Innovate
Consultant
Integrate
Technical Advocate
Innovate / Invest
"Get the right people..."
"doing the right things..."
"within the right framework..."
Innovate
Invest
Integrate
The I0-P Model™
RESULT
I-Operations Realized
"I-Operations creates"
BENEFIT
Sustainable Impact in the Internet Economy
INTERNET ECONOMY
I-Operations

Chapter 3

Challenge

Create Sustainable Impact in the Internet Economy

The Internet Economy does not come without challenges. Those corporations that experience difficulty entering into the Internet Economy often do so because they are operating from a set of false assumptions. Our research indicates that the biggest hindrance to I-Operations is Legacy "Old Economy" Thinking.

Challenges to change

In our qualitative interviews with executives, we asked them to identify the key challenges that organizations face as they integrate Internet technologies into their Operating Models. One point that came up repeatedly was that acquiring the technology was not necessarily the biggest challenge, but rather changing the mind-sets of leaders and people within the organization.

Statement | **Survey**

Lack of vision is a significant hindrance to developing I-Operations.

Lack of knowledge of Internet technologies is a significant hindrance to investing in Internet and network technologies.

The greatest inhibitor of product innovation is legacy systems.

The greatest inhibitor of product innovation is legacy people.

What is it about conventional business wisdom that will get us into trouble in the Internet Economy? This chapter addresses some of the most important challenges to establishing I-Operations.

Challenge 1: Know the details of your Operating Model

We have observed that many companies get bogged down because of the overwhelming challenges of information overload, the rapid pace of technological change, and the foreign economics of some Internet businesses. They have abandoned strategic planning, and have been reluctant to deal with the mundane task of creating an end-to-end Operating Model. But every corporation has an Operating Model. Not all organizations have articulated them well, and some even look with disdain on "getting too organized" and pride themselves on "just doing it." The second and third waves of the Internet were awash with this philosophy. The ads aired during the 2000 Super Bowl attested to the fact that it was better to be cool than coherent. By the time the 2000 Olympics came around, the advertising of companies like United Parcel Service had abruptly shifted to the "we actually do stuff" message. By Super Bowl 2001, the Dot-com was all but "dot-gone;" of the 20 Dot-com advertisers in 2000, only three remained in 2001... and there were no new entries.

This reluctance to formalize Operating Models is nothing new, but the temptation to ignore Operating Models has increased radically. The first reason is part fear and part philosophy. The sages say to make decisions with 10% of the information you need and don't sweat the small stuff. We claim that the absence of a viable and articulated Operating Model will guarantee failure in the New Economy.

Another reason why executives avoid formalizing Internet-enabled Operating Models is their own fear of not appearing competent. A third reason is the avoidance of scrutiny. Until Operating Models are articulated, they are hardly open to challenge. The net result of uncodified Operating Models is that large corporations become hostage to their past, and new corporations become captive to the quirks of their founders.

Challenge 2: Recognize the new value chain

Old World Value Chain

Value chain analysis is helpful to organizations as they analyze the series of things that go into creating goods. It is basically a linear look at the food chain of corporations. As the service level of an industry increases, the value chain is lengthened to include customer-facing segments. Value chains are useful for analyzing certain aspects of corporations, but they reflect the stove-piped view of corporations that was a legacy of 20th Century organizational theory.

In the Internet Economy, this serial process seldom holds true. The creation of value is far more dynamic. Customers and competitors alike are often part of the process. Knowledge workers insert themselves in processes as and when needed. A customer query, suggestion, or critique is

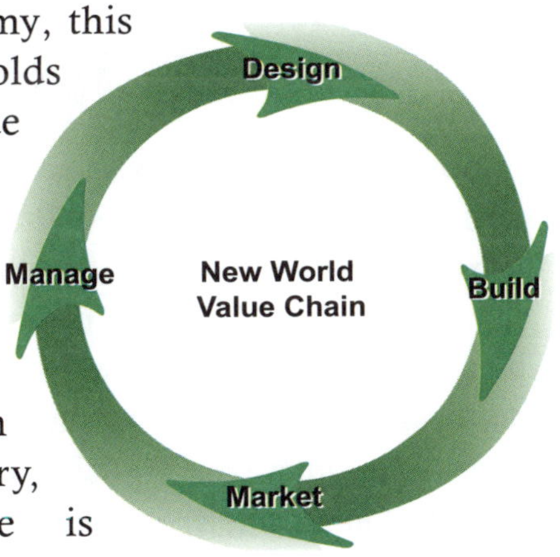

dynamically routed to the right domain expert without regard for internal or external corporate boundaries. This approach is dictated by network technologies and related cultural expectations of accessibility to expertise and information.

In short, value chains are no longer straight lines.

Challenge 3: Eliminate segmented systems

Not surprisingly, the management of information and the related software applications (Information Architectures and Applications Architectures) came to mirror this serial

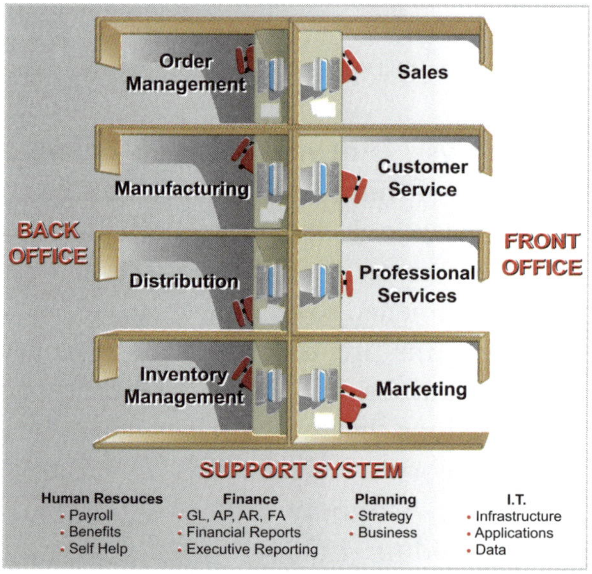

model of the business. Then came a wave of "business reengineering" in the mid-1990s that sought to eliminate this departmentalized view. The elaborate processes of a business that had evolved over the years—particularly those that existed in multiple departments—were mapped out on endless pads of flip chart paper on conference room walls. Slash-and-burn artists quickly identified those processes that could be eliminated, and the related organization structures were similarly trimmed. Some of it was excellent work, but much of it was questionable. The point here is not to debate the merits or demerits of process redesign, but to convey out that it could not have happened without a key enabling technology, the relational database. Shared data, readily and simultaneously accessible to multiple departments across the corporation, enabled people to think about processes and people differently.

But even after all the reengineering had come and gone, the heart of an organization was still segmented into back end and customer-facing functions. There might be a central repository, maybe even a data warehouse, where people with the right front ends, permissions, and training might be able to get to data. But the fundamental view of the application building blocks was split three ways: customer-facing, manufacturing and distribution, and central services (such as Finance and Human Resources). This segmentation does not hold true in the Internet Economy.

Challenge 4: Excel at more than one Value Discipline

Just a few years ago, corporations achieved impact by juggling three areas: 1) product features/quality, 2) price/efficiencies, and 3) service. Several well-respected authors have documented their views that a corporation can excel in one or two of these areas, but never all three. The under-performing corporations were those that promised the unbelievable: best products, at the lowest price, with the best service. They lacked focus and were in no-man's land, offering nothing unique. The market leaders were those that could offer a "good deal" with focus. For example, they might offer superb product functionality with low price, but provide mediocre service. How did they deliver this focused offer? They deployed a single-threaded Operating Model.

Does this rationale hold true in the Internet Era? We learned from our research and experience that an end-to-end Operating Model must be fully aligned and integrated for it to create sustainable impact. This is in part due to the changing nature of value propositions themselves, as noted earlier. The value disciplines approach is a useful tool for analyzing what a corporation has to offer, but it is an inadequate system for generating operating success in the New Economy. The I-Operations approach manifests value delivery in all three areas.

Challenge 5: Resist the naturally evolving Operating Model

Both traditional companies and Internet businesses have afforded themselves the luxury of believing that their Operating Models will evolve over time. Inherent in this practice is a notion that it is acceptable to ignore certain aspects of operations until a later stage in the business cycle. Viewed through the lens of The 10-P Model, we can reevaluate the fundamental assumptions about traditional business life cycles and stages of development. The following series of charts shows the results of an Impact Assessment™, a 360-degree look at a corporation measuring

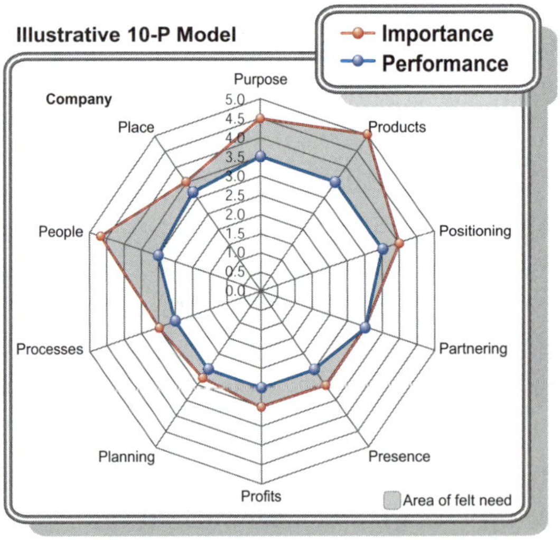

Desired Impact vs. Current Impact across the 10-Ps, which we have identified as the ten components of a well-rounded Operating Model. The first chart shows a company that is

"engineering driven" and has decided to wait until it has its products complete (which they seldom are) before tackling marketing and sales. They perceive a gap or need in the Product area, with People being a close second; "We need more engineers". In reality, business processes are lacking, but the engineers feel that "anyone can do that stuff" and the Process gap goes undetected for a while. They perceive their next hire to be "a sales guy" who can sell all the cool stuff they have nearly finished developing.

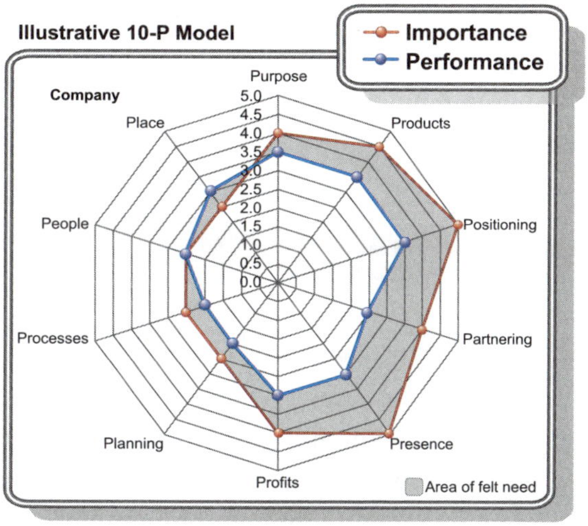

This engineering-skewed view either results in a lack of a marketing and sales competency being established, or the engineers become sales people (with varying degrees of success), and the product development suffers.

Marketing driven start-ups are different because they are focused on their external world from the outset. Because they have little regard for institutionalizing internal processes, they feel their need is in the customer-facing or external Ps. The theory is that they will build-out the back office later—Process, People, Planning, Place and Profit. In a number of Dot-com cases, the companies wasted millions of dollars on marketing well in advance of having a technology patent filed or a product developed. The Impact Assessment for

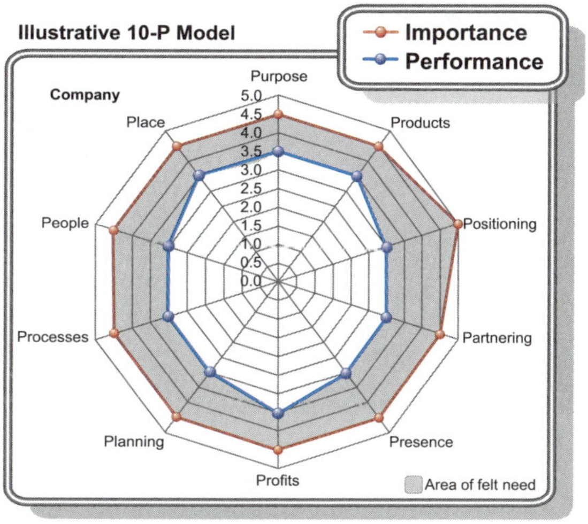

marketing-driven corporations therefore reflects a strongly-felt need around Presence, Positioning and Partnering. They have little regard for the remaining Ps, unless they are "hiring like crazy." In that case, they also have a felt need around People. Here the death spiral comes when the products and services that enthused sales people have been promising fail to arrive, and the confidence of internal and external stakeholders is shaken. For those with proven products, the same can be true when e-commerce sales of old products—cars, CDs, clothing, whatever—fail to materialize.

JDS UNIPHASE Revenue (In Billions)

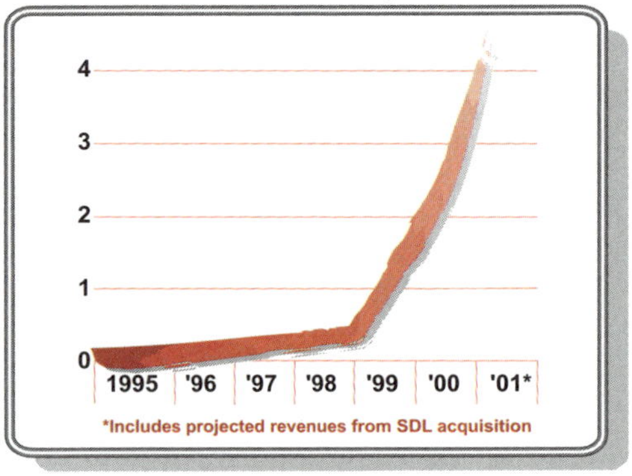

Thus far there has been no mention of profits. But when corporations reach the Growth phase of the business life cycle, the corporation typically becomes more aware of inefficiencies and gaps in core business processes. The upside is that this creates impetus to build infrastructure; the downside is that if there is no clear organizing principle behind the push to fill out the Operating Model, a corporation can entrench bad models. Further, in the attempt to become efficient, they can lose their cutting edge with clients. The gaps in the Impact Assessment are therefore evenly spread between internal and external Ps. Unless there is a dynamic sales and distribution capability that keeps the sales engine running, there is a danger of

JUNIPER NETWORKS Revenue (In Millions)

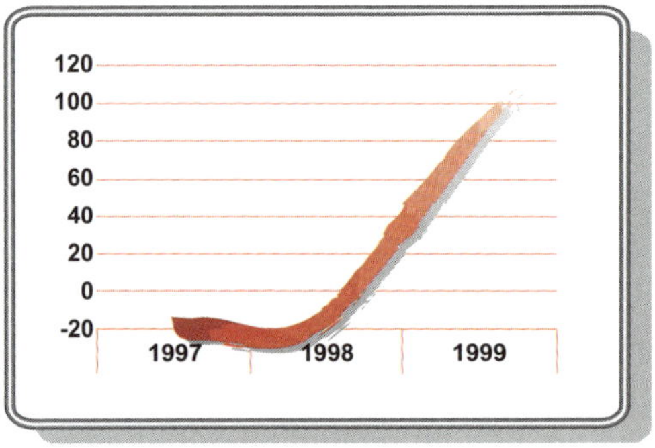

atrophying prior to achieving a level of operational excellence. In a worst-case scenario, the corporation institutionalizes processes and procedures that were not well founded to begin with. The Impact Assessment then reveals a company that is stuck in the middle with general gaps in all 10-Ps. In an attempt to become efficient, they can easily lose their cutting edge with clients and enter into decline.

The Internet does not resolve the gaps in the Operating Model. If there is no cohesive framework, it can cause the gaps to become apparent more quickly. The Internet is a win-fast, fail-fast environment, and the notion of self-evolving Operating Models is risky. Over the average shelf life of a traditional corporation, there used to be time for reinvention in response to changing market conditions. The rate of change in the Internet world eliminates this luxury. The J-curve or Hockey Stick curve means that high growth corporations transition from needing little infrastructure to requiring large, scalable infrastructure in a matter of months. A look at some of Cisco's peers during the six months before and after "first customer ship" illustrates this fact (refer to charts on previous page JDS Uniphase, Juniper Networks). It also points out that one cannot afford to wait until the growth stage to think about architecture for the end-to-end Operating Model.

Application Service Provider. ASP—An organization that hosts software applications on its own servers within its own facilities. Customers access the application via private lines or the Internet. Also called a "commercial service provider".

Fortunately, Application Service Providers (ASPs) can be a stop-gap for many of these companies. In essence, these vendors allow a company to outsource their integration challenge. This does not take away the need for a corporation to begin thinking about end-to-end operations from day one, or perhaps day two. The myth that claims that you can get to that back end stuff later is just that, a myth. For many such companies, later is too late.

Partnering and the Internet

Our research indicated that companies with I-Operations are successfully leveraging Internet technologies to implement partnering strategies and manage partners. In essence, they are using Internet/network-based technologies to communicate with partners which includes sharing inventory management and ordering capabilities. Ultimately, Internet based tools are reducing the barriers that have traditionally existed between organizations. Furthermore, partnering in the New Economy has not only become more efficient, but has enabled organizations to focus on their core competencies by making it easier and more cost efficient to outsource those functions that do not fall within the domain of the organization's core competency. A good example of this is Cisco Systems, who, by leveraging their ecosystem of partners, is able to focus on their core competency of designing and developing products.

Statement | **Survey Results**

Internet-based technologies make it easier to identify, build and leverage an ecosystem of partners.

We leverage Internet technologies to manage partners.

Challenge 6: Form partnerships

Over the past five years, many books have been written about Partnering, such as *The Death of Competition*, *Co-opetition*, and *Getting Partnering Right*. However, forming partnerships is difficult and generally fails to live up to expectations. That does not mean that you can make it on your own. A key to the Internet Economy is figuring out the partners you need to help you create sustainable impact.

"Partnering is absolutely necessary for survival and is significantly more difficult than acquisitions," says John Chambers, President and CEO of Cisco Systems. Cisco has made over 60 acquisitions and has held minority positions in more than 70 companies (through October 2000).[12]

Yet its number of strategic partnerships is less than 10. That is quite a record for a relatively young company. Obviously, John speaks from experience.

Challenge 7: Build the infrastructure

Cisco hosts about 1,000 customer visits each quarter in their executive briefing centers. Many are customers who come with good questions and great ideas. Some are pioneers in the Internet Economy, others are still wondering what it means to them. Beyond the specific industry or business problem that is under discussion, we see the unspoken question: "How do I infuse network technologies into my Operating Model?" Our response involves a combination of ten dynamic facets of business that encompasses people, culture, communications, vision and values. Buying the technology and building your infrastructure is critical, but it does not guarantee success! However, you cannot participate in the current revolution unless you buy or build the enabling technologies. Buying the technology may not guarantee a winner's position, but it does get you in the game.

In our research we found many companies that were willing to describe themselves as having I-Operations. In fact, 92% of all respondents said that they had deployed Internet -related technologics. And 66% said that these technologies provided them with a competitive advantage.[13] An average of those two statistics indicates that approximately 80% of U.S. corporations believe they are participating in the Internet Economy. However, relatively few were prepared to say that their competitors would acknowledge that they have achieved a competitive advantage through I-Operations. In fact, using this question from our survey as the acid test, we find that only 20% of the U.S. companies actually are participating.[14] We are also concerned that many corporations from all domains—academia, business, government and philanthropy—are clutching at straws in the absence of a cohesive approach to applying the Internet to their core business. In our opinion, you are in a precarious position as a company if you believe you have I-Operations when, in fact, you do not! Technology alone is not the answer.

Challenge 8: Move fast, stay open

In most situations, customers want to be thought of as more than just customers. However, businesses and individual consumers all desire fair pricing, good service, and excellent products. The challenge, in this time of

Stakeholder interaction

The increased ability to communicate with stakeholders is a clear benefit of Internet applications. Our research indicates that I-Operations companies have the ability to more efficiently interact with external stakeholders. It is likely that as technology develops, there will be newer and better applications deployed to further integrate information flows between companies within an ecosystem.

Statement **Survey Results**

Internet-enabled applications have enabled us to more efficiently interact with:

- Customers

- Suppliers

- Distributors

- Partners

- Investors

automated B2B transactions, is to make the customer your partner, or at the least your client (denoting a continuing and repeating relationship).

Clients today expect access to information and service 24 hours a day, 7 days a week. If I desire to configure my router, order a new book, or arrange financing on an automobile purchase at 3 A.M. on Saturday morning, the business must be open! Similarly, if I need pre-sale or post-sale support at similar times, it must be there.

The wealth of information available over the Internet has grown tremendously over the last five years and does not appear to be slowing any time soon. Never before have we had a more informed consumer than today. On the other hand, never before have you had a more informed competitor! This information on the Internet is available to them, also. It enables your competition to maneuver and respond at a much quicker pace. Of course the quid pro quo is that you also maneuver and respond more rapidly. Internet time is a reality, and it is epidemic.

Intensified competition, a more informed client who expects a continuous quality interface, and the resulting Internet time creates a most challenging business environment. You've never had a better excuse for hypertension.

These challenges merit a response, and the response should be aimed at creating sustainable impact in the Internet Economy. To achieve this, we believe I-Operations is mandatory.

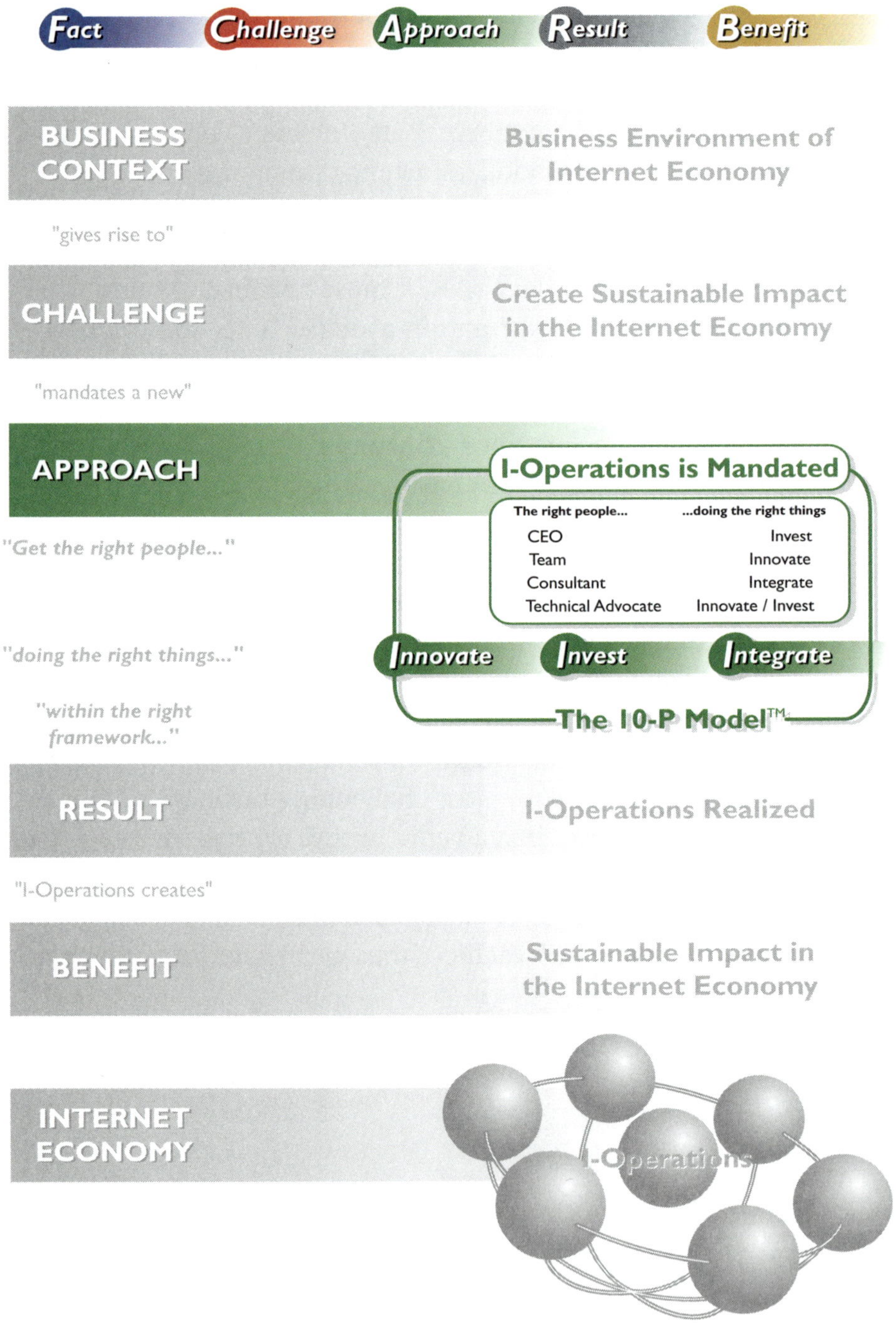
Fact
Challenge
Approach
Result
Benefit
BUSINESS CONTEXT
Business Environment of Internet Economy
"gives rise to"
CHALLENGE
Create Sustainable Impact in the Internet Economy
"mandates a new"
APPROACH
I-Operations is Mandated
The right people...
...doing the right things
CEO
Invest
Team
Innovate
Consultant
Integrate
Technical Advocate
Innovate / Invest
"Get the right people..."
"doing the right things..."
"within the right framework..."
Innovate
Invest
Integrate
The 10-P Model™
RESULT
I-Operations Realized
"I-Operations creates"
BENEFIT
Sustainable Impact in the Internet Economy
INTERNET ECONOMY
I-Operations

Chapter 4

Approach

I-Operations Mandated

Organizations have always done well when all aspects of their operations are aligned behind a central purpose. This is no less true in the Internet Age. It can, however, be a more daunting task precisely because of the verbal hype that has accompanied Internet-related business. Our research validates the importance of understanding one's core business—with and without the Internet. Initial interviews included companies that ranged from the "pure Internet plays" to the legacy "brick and mortar" establishments. It soon became apparent that those who were having success in the New Economy understood the basics of their business, with or without the Internet.

Pure Internet Play. A corporation whose business could not exist outside of the Internet.

Beyond that, successful companies were able to grasp the implications of the Internet for their total, end-to-end operations. They could clearly make the statement: "This is my core business; this is my core business on the Internet."

In particular, successful executives had either a conscious or an intuitive grasp of the broad reach of their Operating Model. They avoided the "and then a miracle happens" scenario that plagued many of their peers in the early part of 2000.

Internet strategy is business strategy

We found that the businesses that had successfully integrated I-Operations into their Operating Model didn't differentiate between business strategy and Internet strategy. They were one and the same, as they had developed an end-to-end view of the Operating Model when it came to integrating Internet /network-enabled technologies.

A common misconception among the remaining companies is that they believe that they are a legitimate player in the Internet Economy if they simply have a website. Our litmus test for determining if an organization is or is not a part of the New Economy is whether or not they have deployed a New World Application to significant advantage. Commonly, the answer to this question was "No" (or negative), but to the question of whether or not they were a player in the New Economy, the same respondents answered "Yes" (or positive).

Statement

We recognize that Internet strategy is really business strategy.

Survey Results

The title of this book was born out of what we have learned. A business must have I-Operations (an Internet-enabled Operating Model) in order to compete. I-Operations encompasses the concept of the virtual enterprise. A virtual enterprise breaks down traditional barriers that inhibit information access through an intra-company hierarchy. It opens up the company, helping it share the critical information and decision-making authority with external partners, distributors, customers, and suppliers, as well as internally with employees and employee groups. Under the auspices of a virtual enterprise, applications are deployed using Internet technologies to significantly improve the bottom line or market share of a company. These applications are called New World Applications.

Entering new markets enabled by the Internet and I-Operations certainly qualifies as gaining market share, and is one of the most noted benefits of New World Applications.

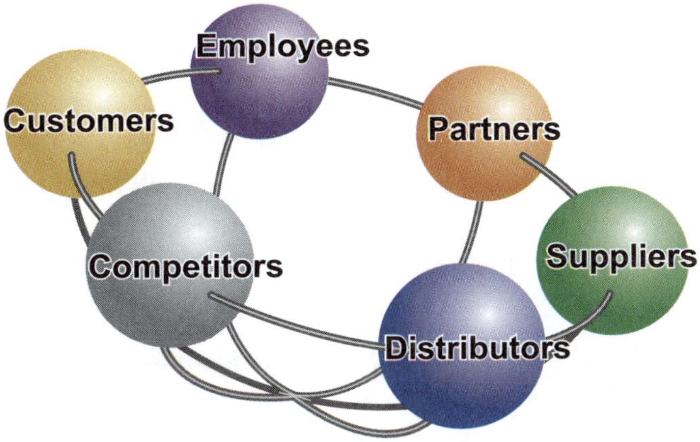

Today we find ourselves in an environment stimulated by I-Operations enterprises. For those participating, it is encouraging that they are still in the minority (less than 20%, as noted earlier) and thus have a significant market lead. However, a precarious situation exists in that almost 80% of companies in the U.S. believe they are proactive participants in this.[15] This belief is based on their actual or intended deployment of a network-based application. However, without positive bottom line impact or market share increase, it is not participation, it is delusion! If your competitors do not recognize your applications as significant, then they most likely are not.

The business environment today is labeled an Internet Economy. This Internet Economy is fueled by the communication capabilities embodied in the Internet. Its pace is harrowing, and consumers expect anywhere, anytime business operations. I-Operations extends the concept of the virtual enterprise and is already being successfully deployed by the leading enterprises. Others must learn how to participate or be left behind, at considerable business risk. It is indeed an exciting time to be in business!

With the emergence of the Internet comes an opportunity to take business integration to another level. Fundamental changes in the traditional divisions between front office, back office, and support systems are now possible. Early on, the Web was utilized primarily as a marketing tool. It provided a platform from which organizations could publish information about themselves and their products or services. At this stage, it was obvious to many observers that we were just scratching the surface of what we would soon come to call the Internet Economy. As the Internet grew and technology enabled e-commerce capabilities, the potential of the Web was unleashed in a transformational way. An explosion of Business-to-Consumer companies occurred, and it seemed as though any new Dot-com company could compete with traditional brick and mortar companies. More recently, the vast potential of Business-to-Business e-commerce was recognized, and models were developed to take advantage of the resulting opportunities.

Operating Models are changing

The purpose of the Operating Model is to deliver on the value proposition. It is clear that we are in a time of fundamental change, and it is apparent that the Internet can have a profound effect on the Operating Models of organizations. It is yet to be determined who the winners will be or exactly what the Internet Economy will look like. Instead of focusing on a particular Internet Economy model for specific industries, we will explore the impact of the Internet on end-to-end operations of an organization. Our scope includes more than Internet companies, and our analysis is relevant to all organizations that hope to exist in the years ahead.

Our experience and research shows that all of this is changing in major ways. By way of overview:

- Internet-enabled technology is transforming every facet of the Operating Model.

- The line between front office and back office functions is blurring.
- All aspects of an organization's Operating Model are becoming visible, if not transparent, to external stakeholders.
- Internal stakeholders similarly have a view into an organization's core functions.
- All functions (and their supporting applications) have the potential of being customer-facing, thanks, in most part, to Internet technologies.

External stakeholders. Individuals or organizations that are outside of the corporation and have a stake in its success or failure. These include, but are not limited to, customers, shareholders, boards, distributors, suppliers and partners.

Internal stakeholders. Those parties internal to a corporation who contribute to and benefit from the well being of the corporation.

Exploring these statements a bit further, 83% of the executives we interviewed strongly agreed with this statement: "The line between front office and back office functions is blurring."[16] Historically, a layer of people stood between the customer and the back end systems such as manufacturing and distribution. Now customers have the ability to track the status of their orders using standard Web interfaces. In addition, companies are able to effectively incorporate customers into the design process. For example, TrueSan.com allows you to design your storage area network, Levi Strauss your blue jeans. For some companies with whom we spoke, the product cannot actually be delivered without the Internet. EA.com, is an online gaming company spun off by Electronic Arts that develops, manages, distributes and delivers its product over the Internet. No Internet, no company.

The key point is that the Internet enables customers to reach into core applications of the business—design, manufacturing, accounting, distribution, etc.—and these systems are therefore as customer-facing as sales, marketing and customer service. In other words, all Web-enabled

Operating Models are becoming more customer-facing

As we analyzed the Operating Models of organizations with I-Operations, it became clear that the Operating Model is becoming more visible to all parties, both internal to the organization as well as external. Internally, I-Operations companies are utilizing Intranet technologies to manage employees and to empower them with company information and client management applications. Externally, customers are able to access information that was not readily available prior to Internet-enabled operating models. Self-serve access to account information, order status and package tracking has given customers the ability to see deeper into the Operating Model than ever before. Suppliers and distributors similarly have a heightened level of connectivity, which has resulted in increased information flows between all players in the value chain. With better information comes the ability to manage, plan and support the product flows between organizations.

Statement **Survey Results**

We enable customers to see deeper into the back end operations of the company via Internet technologies.

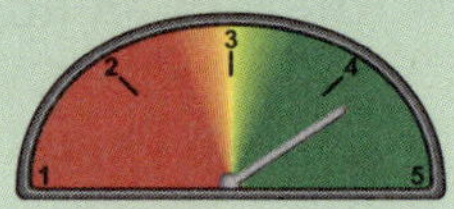

The Internet enables operating models to be more customer-facing.

The boundaries between front and back office systems are being deliberately erased.

Internet/network-based technologies enable us to remove process inefficiencies at the borders between organizations.

applications are customer-facing, and the distinction between front and back end systems will ultimately disappear. This should change our approach to investments, and it should change the way that Information Technology professionals define the various layers of their organization's architecture, namely, the Applications Architecture, Data Architecture, Communications Architecture, and Technology Architecture.

The fact that external stakeholders—shareholders, customers, competitors, suppliers—have a greater view into the corporation implies that we have to be more deliberate about aligning the internal and external views of our company's information. This sounds easier than it is, because we are also in a time when digital technologies readily blur the lines between reality and fiction. When you add imagination to technology, you might find yourself asking, "What do we want our story to be?" We interviewed an individual who, when asked what job he did at a company, said, "You know our advertisement about the person who does x and y… well, I'm trying to build the system to make that happen." We call this "strategy-by-advertising." At the same time, Internet technologies will allow external stakeholders to find out who you really are: "What actually happened to that order, is the check really in the mail, did you really put in a trouble ticket or service order, and does the self-service customer service really work?" It is, therefore, essential to have a strategy and an execution plan that ensures that all components of the Operating Model are consistent, integrated and aligned.

Information about an organization is visible to internal stakeholders, and this alters the organizational or people component of Operating Models. The historical rationale for having hierarchical organizations—someone with more information needs to make the decision—is fading fast. Similarly, it is easier for staff to work outside the defined boundaries of their department, because physical barriers do not confine the flow of ideas, conversations and functional relationships. This also challenges the way in which people "add value" in that contributions of intellectual capital, while more intangible, are more transparent. Questions are, therefore, raised about our traditional views of the architecture of organizations themselves. We will explore these later on.

Ten Drivers of Impact

Every organization exists to have an impact. We indicated earlier that a complex set of factors goes into the creation of an organization's impact. Because the Internet exacerbates the successes and failures of corporations, they must have a complete understanding of what drives impact today. By prior analysis, The Institute has identified Ten Drivers of Impact. Each of these plays a role in shaping what defines an organization, what they offer to their target audience, and how they are organized. You can think of these as ten spokes in a wheel, each one being essential to strength and long-term effectiveness.

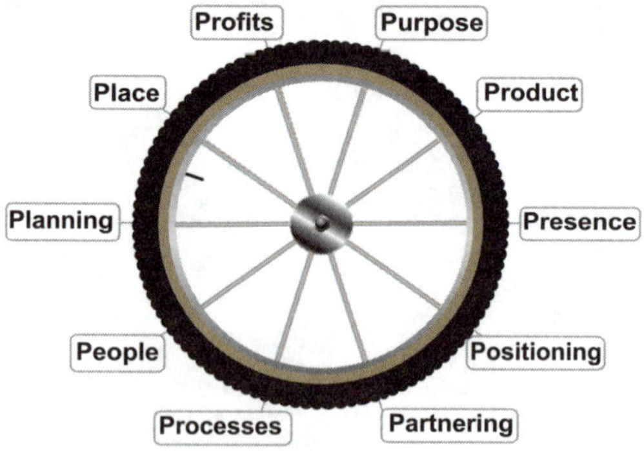

These ten Impact-drivers have been shaped into a proprietary model, and this model has been successful with start-ups, Fortune 100 companies, academic and non-profit organizations. We structured our I-Operations research using this ten-spoked model. While this research commenced before the Dot-com downturn that began in April 2000, this "market correction" supports our conclusions. Companies that roll the dice and create value propositions that are not backed by integrated Operating Models are at risk, precisely because they ignore some of the Ten Drivers of Impact. In fact, we believe many of these failures were the result of faulty execution.

For Example:

- Over the 1999 Christmas shopping season, a slew of e-tailers sold products that they could not deliver. They had sales; they lacked fulfillment capabilities. They had the front end technology, but had not effectively deployed the back end technology to support it.

- Boo.com is an example of a company that had implemented an elaborate back end system, but lacked an integrated and useable front end.
  In May of 2000, after months of promising to revolutionize the face of e-commerce, Boo went out of business. "Boo was so convinced it was changing the world of e-commerce that it overlooked the truth that working technology matters more than fancy features."[17] Boo developed an elaborate back end system that was designed to handle multiple currencies, multiple languages, on-the-fly tax calculations, and integration with multiple fulfillment partners.
  On the front end, Boo had developed an elaborate website with all the bells and whistles. But it was so elaborate that it ran over schedule by more than

> five months and only worked with the latest browsers with the latest plug-ins. In addition, it wasn't Mac-compatible. The website had 3D capabilities, zoom-in features, and was able to model its products on virtual mannequins. The cost for all of this technology is rumored to be between $47 and $53 million. The reason for Boo's demise was not lack of technology, but lack of alignment between front end and back end. Boo concentrated too intently on image. It played to the media, it spent money on treating its more than 400 employees extravagantly, and it focused almost entirely on presence. It forgot about the other Drivers of Impact and the importance of bringing them all into alignment. After the collapse of Boo, an employee intelligently stated, "No matter how good your back end systems are, the user will only remember your front end. Fail there, and you fail, period."[18] The reverse, however, is also true.

So what are the Ten Drivers of Impact? They also happen to be the ten components of The 10-P Model. We will outline these components here, and later tackle what an end-to-end Operating Model might look like "on the Internet."

Driver of Impact	Explanation
Purpose	The purpose of an organization—including its identity and values—radically affects the ability of that organization to have an impact. Many organizations spend countless months laboring over clarifying their products, when what they are lacking is a purpose. Others have a stated purpose but lack clarity on the values that are essential to fulfilling the purpose.

Products

Products and services are key components of how the customer—or target audience—experiences the organization. Products create the "touch, see, and smell" factors that make an organization come alive. For non-profits and service organizations, products often take the form of programs.

Presence

Products consumed out of context do not carry the full impact that the purveyor intends. Traditionally, marketing is intended to make consumers aware of their needs and how particular products can fill those needs. Marketing creates presence, a mind-set for the product or corporation, and it builds a story and experience that goes beyond the simple consumption of the product. Presence results in impact.

Positioning

If another corporation creates an advantage (even if only in the perception of customers) then purpose, products and presence will not be enough. Establishing a clear positioning of both organization and products is essential. The value proposition of the corporation and what differentiates it from others is essential to creating impact.

Partnering

Numerous books and publications have touted the benefits of partnering in the past five years. The attempts at partnering have not occurred out of mutual admiration and togetherness. Customers have simply demanded it, and increasingly made it a condition of business that suppliers cooperate. Why? Because they know that no one company can do everything well. Partnering creates better impact for corporations and their customers alike.

Before continuing with the list, we want to point out that prior to the advent of I-Operations, we used to refer to the five Ps we have just reviewed as the customer-facing Ps or external Ps. It was easy to argue that the customer was exposed to the products, marketing and competitive messaging of the company—and to some degree, to their partners. Since undertaking this research, we can no longer refer to the 'external Ps' and the 'internal Ps', because the Internet creates the very real possibility that all facets of the corporation are now visible to internal and external stakeholders. All 10-Ps can be customer-facing.

Driver of Impact	Explanation
Processes	Conventional wisdom used to state that "Process is king," for operationally excellent organizations. Process certainly is a Driver of Impact, but this is true for all corporations. Core business processes can either be handled just efficiently, or they can be deliberately directed towards the creation of impact. Another aspect of business processes is decision-making. With the ever increasing information component of products, the location, speed, and quality of decision-making processes are influencing customers' perceptions of value.
People	If there is a line of sight from each person in the organization to the external customers of the organization, people can have a tremendous effect on the impact of the corporation. When the people—including the way in which they are organized—are thoroughly aligned with the purpose of the corporation, impact is heightened.

Place	A company's location, the feel of the facilities, the corporate identity that goes beyond buildings, proximity to customers, partners, and others in one's ecosystem… all these can be used in the place spoke of the Impact Wheel. This is no less true for virtual corporations. The philosophy of Place is true for conventional and click-based corporations.
Planning	We are just emerging from an era—albeit a short one—where the mantra was: "Planning is for wimps." Real executives, we were told, make huge decisions on a sniff of information and raw intuition. Strategic thinking went from a long-term outlook to, "How do we do what our advertising says we do?" Appropriate planning—not "Strategy by Advertising"—is still a crucial Driver of Impact. The old adage is true: "If you fail to plan, you plan to fail." Unfortunately, our convention-denying world doesn't place planners in the cover stories too often.
Profit	The economic model of a corporation—not just the measurement of profit, but how income is generated—is clearly essential. Over-simplification in this area spells disaster for many companies. ("We acquire customers—lots of them—and then a miracle happens.") Transitioning profit from an accounting tool to a strategic weapon is the habit of champions. While a larger bottom line is not the aim of every organization, sustainable impact is best achieved in concert with sustainable economics.

We will use The 10-P Model throughout this book to ensure that our coverage of I-Operations is cohesive and complete.

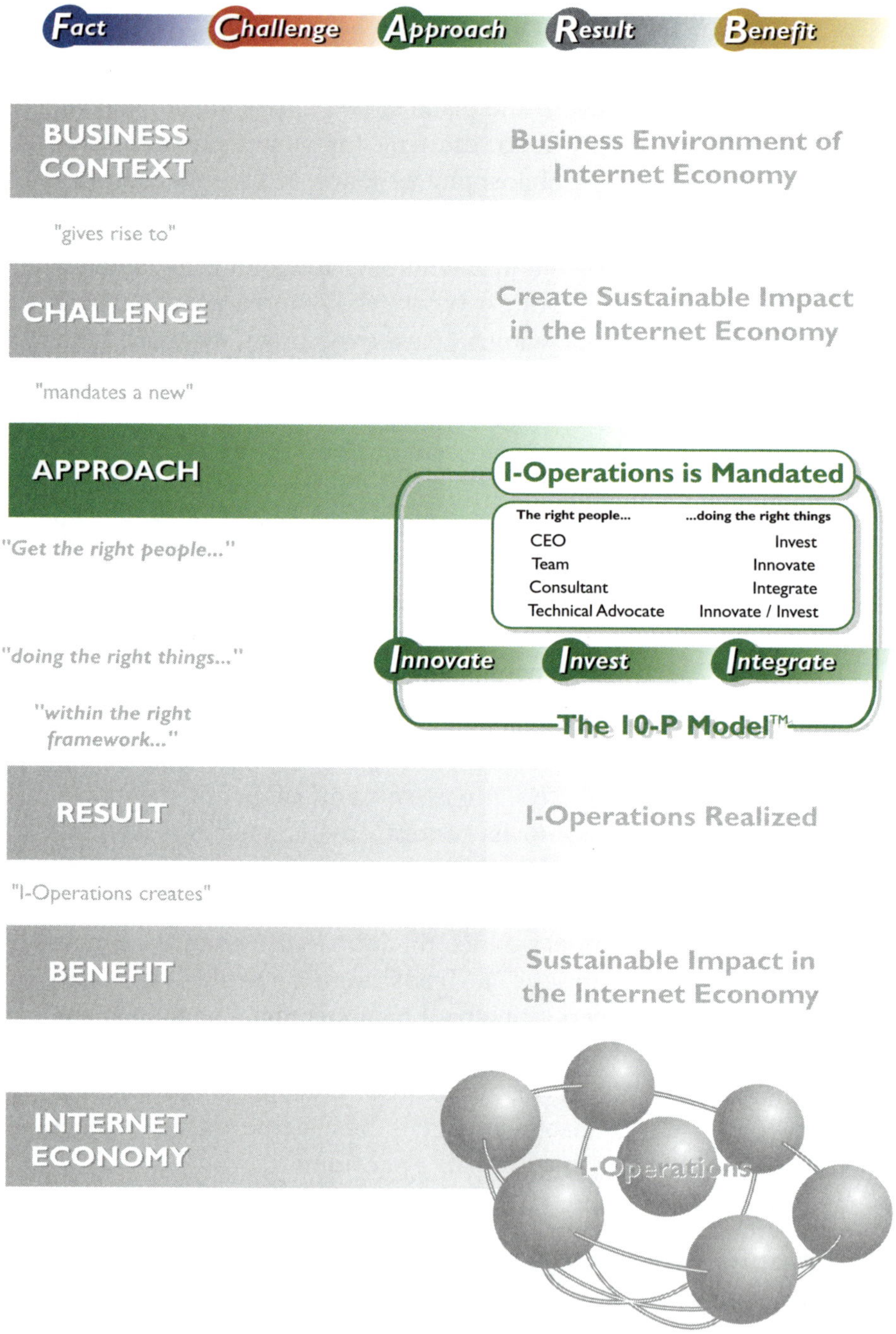
Fact
Challenge
Approach
Result
Benefit
BUSINESS CONTEXT
Business Environment of Internet Economy
"gives rise to"
CHALLENGE
Create Sustainable Impact in the Internet Economy
"mandates a new"
APPROACH
I-Operations is Mandated
The right people...
...doing the right things
CEO
Invest
Team
Innovate
Consultant
Integrate
Technical Advocate
Innovate / Invest
"Get the right people..."
"doing the right things..."
"within the right framework..."
Innovate
Invest
Integrate
The 10-P Model™
RESULT
I-Operations Realized
"I-Operations creates"
BENEFIT
Sustainable Impact in the Internet Economy
INTERNET ECONOMY
I-Operations

Chapter 5

Approach

I-Operations: Innovation

It is hard to deny that the Internet has resulted in radical changes in some businesses. It has also spawned new ventures across the business, academic and social service sectors. We have seen wild ideas turned into businesses that otherwise would never have come into being.

A driving factor is that the Internet has unleashed innovation while simultaneously either enabling or benefiting from important trends. When helping clients develop strategy, The Institute performs what it calls "Trend Sanity Checks" to ensure that the proposed strategies are moving in the same direction as the trends. Trends by their very nature have to be monitored and updated. We urge you to keep your own Trend Bank relevant to your specific situations, making sure that it covers a holistic array of categories that include corporate, personal, technology, political and economic trends, to name a handful. If the strategy you are considering is Internet-based innovation across your entire Operating Model, how well do you think it aligns with this sample of trends?

> **"Innovators and men of genius have almost always been regarded as fools at the beginning (and very often at the end) of their careers."**
> Fyodor Dostoyevsky

> **"He that will not apply new remedies must expect new evils; for time is the greatest innovator."**
> Francis Bacon

TREND SANITY CHECK

Is your strategy counter to or consistent with major trends?

Counter To	TREND	Consistent With
○	From Government-controlled to Market-driven	☐
○	From Labor-intensive to high technology	☐
○	From male dominance to the emergence of women	☐
○	From West to East	☐
○	Globalization	☐
○	The shifting location of education: home, religious institution, government, corporation	☐
○	Cashing out	☐
○	Cashing in	☐
○	Home-based business	☐
○	From serial career management to complex life management	☐
○	Roll-your-own community	☐
○	Rediscovery of roots	☐
○	Innovation in small packages	☐
○	What we might do tomorrow doesn't exist today	☐
○	Worldwide leverage for home-grown ideas	☐
○	Knowledge	☐
○	Digitization	☐
○	Virtualization	☐
○	Molecularization	☐
○	Integration	☐

Regardless of the economy, every week business and technology publications contain promises of the "new, new thing," and many of these are technology based.

Perhaps a more important reason why the Internet has unleashed creativity is that it has freed people to think differently. For corporations who are serving customers, this opens up possibilities of goods and services that even five years ago would never have flown. The flip side is that the expectations of customers have skyrocketed. That brings us full circle back to the question of Operating Models. What Operating Model is needed to design, build, market and manage the "best deal" for your target audience?

Even before the Internet heated up, a few enlightened corporations created a stepping-stone that moved them beyond the single-minded "value disciplines" approach. In the mid-90s a handful of companies began to wonder whether they could compete across two disciplines if they partnered with others. Successful companies began to explore alliances as a means of fighting on two fronts. For example:

- LL Bean teamed with Federal Express to do fulfillment.

- Dell outsourced manufacturing and logistics to achieve Operational Excellence.

But the basic strategy remained the same: focus on one area, get it right, and outsource the peripheral processes. The rigid or static Operating Models that were the unglamorous underpinnings of these successful corporations were behind this strategy. Furthermore, the characteristics of each Operating Model were radically different under each value discipline.

Then came Internet speed.

With all of the logic about value disciplines, companies assumed they had to attain parity in their secondary disciplines. As your competitors raised the bar, you could not afford to ignore them. With Internet speed, however, the rate of change in each area is so fast that catching up to parity happens continually. Competitive forces are, therefore, compelling companies to fight on multiple fronts simultaneously.

Then came added complexity.

An effective corporation has to concern itself with many more factors than just product, price and service.

The Institute's 10-P Model is one representation of this added complexity. Having a winning value proposition now means that a corporation has to have all of its Drivers of Impact totally aligned behind its purpose. And given the bias towards misalignment that exists in most organizations, we need frameworks and enabling technologies that capture this complexity.

The combination of visibility, openness and measurability of Internet technologies creates a host of opportunities for innovation that rigid Operating Models would not allow. I-Operations and its related enabling technologies provide the framework for flexible Operating Models. To be an effective company, you therefore have to be based on e-business technologies.

There are numerous examples of corporations utilizing the Internet to expand their value proposition.

- Customer-intimate companies can have greater product selection and radically improved efficiency. Nordstrom, a customer-intimate service provider, has an online shoe catalogue that boasts the largest shoe store in the world.

- Silicon Valley Bank offers online expertise through e-source.
- Operationally excellent companies are becoming customer-intimate solutions providers and product leaders.
- Dell maintains a database of customer configurations, thereby offering 24-hour solutions in the event of failures, and offers a leading-edge selection of products.
- Product Leaders are pushing the envelope of lowest product cost and enjoyable customer experiences.

The days of a single value discipline are over.

Drivers of Impact in an I-Operations world

The 10-P Model applies with or without the Internet. Many corporations that are not Internet-enabled have sound Operating Models, but we are approaching a time when corporations will move from a fragmented view of the Internet to what has been called an e-everywhere view.

> In the next wave, FORTUNE 500 companies will make such a core part of their businesses that the difference between ***e*** and everything else will be nonexistent. Or they won't be in business anymore.[19]

Our qualitative research specifically explores the impact of the Internet on every aspect of an organization's Operating Model. We have gleaned from our findings a composite view of how Old World Operations and I-Operations companies can be different.

Driver of Impact	***Old World Operations***	***I-Operations***
Purpose	• Company-centric: discussed in a way that implied that the corporation's needs came first	• Organization's mission infused with purpose with which employees (Associates) can identify
Products	• Web-stuff tagged on to old products	• Designed from the inside out: web fully integrated into products
Positioning	• Based on Features and Functions	• Based on the company's story, branding and delivering this as a unique customer experience
Presence	• Static • Published, printed	• Interactive, living • Integrated across multiple media
Partnering	• Transactional • At best, supply chain oriented	• Recognizes, builds and leverages an ecosystem • Builds I-Operations that extend beyond the boundaries of one corporation
Process	• Separate processes for e-business	• Ubiquitous E: e-everywhere
Place	• Physical, entrenched, unmovable	• Accessible anywhere with heightened sense of immediacy and closeness • More than office facilities
People	• Organizational fads: centralized, decentralized, teams, hierarchical, flat...	• Flexible organization structure • Connected, continuous communications • Fun, free, fluid
Planning	• Periodic • Static	• Continuous • New measures... continuous measures
Profit	• Web-business secondary • An optional channel	• Web economics integrated into the total financial model

One of the reasons we can venture to embrace the entire Operating Model at once is the transparent and easy flow of information facilitated by Internet technologies. As Michael Dell states,

> Rapid and robust information flow saves time and money. It transforms organizations because it eliminates paper-based functions, flattens organizational layers and integrates global operations.[20]

An example of this is the use of IP Telephony in the hospitality industry. By thinking beyond traditional telephony, hotels can enable customers to order services, report plumbing problems, settle bills and book a tee time, all using their IP telephone in the hotel room. Beyond this, the customer can be assigned a digital identity in the form of a permanently assigned phone number at that hotel chain. This serves both the customer, and will increase customer loyalty.

While not using I-Operations language, Scott McNealy of Sun Microsystems endorses why corporations have to innovate across all dimensions of the Operating Model:

> You have to worry about death by a thousand cuts, which is what the Internet is all about. There's not going to be one big thunderbolt that kills you. If you don't Dot-com your business, if you don't put your employees online, if you don't put your customers online, if you don't put your service data online, each one of those things will come back to get you. Most of these thousand cuts are self-inflicted.[21]

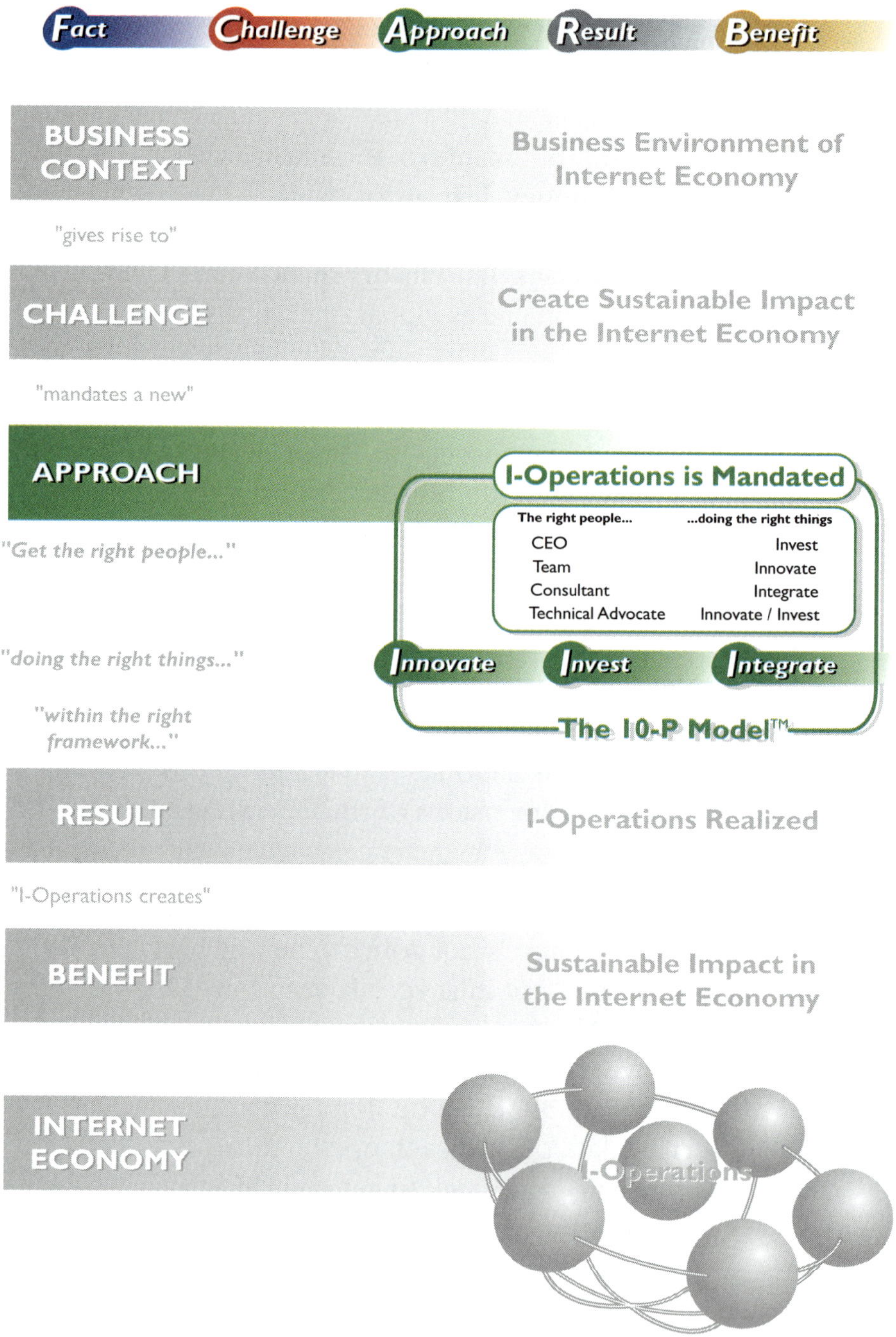
Fact
Challenge
Approach
Result
Benefit
BUSINESS CONTEXT
Business Environment of Internet Economy
"gives rise to"
CHALLENGE
Create Sustainable Impact in the Internet Economy
"mandates a new"
APPROACH
I-Operations is Mandated
The right people...
...doing the right things
CEO
Invest
Team
Innovate
Consultant
Integrate
Technical Advocate
Innovate / Invest
"Get the right people..."
"doing the right things..."
"within the right framework..."
Innovate
Invest
Integrate
The 10-P Model™
RESULT
I-Operations Realized
"I-Operations creates"
BENEFIT
Sustainable Impact in the Internet Economy
INTERNET ECONOMY
I-Operations

Chapter 6

Approach

I-Operations: Investment

In the Year 2000 a steady stream of executives from FORTUNE 500 companies made the pilgrimage to Silicon Valley technology companies in search of a "new, new thing." By 2002 this stream had all but petered out. Constraints on travel and a general caution about new spending on technology left executives in their old dilemma. On the one hand, technology executives are having to prove the business value of IT spending, and many are struggling to do so because they do not have a good grasp of business strategy. On the other hand, the slew of increasingly complex technologies is just as perplexing for business executives as it was before, and many do not understand such technologies. Most of these new technologies are Internet-related, and executives therefore need to have a clear mental framework for sifting through I-Operations investment decisions.

The difficult economic climate of 2001-2002 brought the Investment dilemma into stark relief:

Slash costs... and be poised for growth.

Save money... but don't get behind.

Think "bottom line"... and stay current on critical emerging technologies.

This dilemma is made worse by the language differences between vendors (as they hate to be called) and their customers. Customers are looking to implement not just technology but solutions that deliver real benefit to their corporations. These solutions usually incorporate applications that automate or enhance business processes. Creators of emerging technology often name their tools and technologies "applications," but fail to realize that their customers connote a much richer meaning to that word.

The world of converged communications is a good example of this tension between technology vendors and their clients. Purveyors of IP Telephony technologies that are exciting but "not quite there yet" hope desperately for a "killer application" that will not only validate their technology, but make it irresistible to customers. On the client side, some buyers are cautious, not wanting to end up replacing a functional PBX system with an expensive IP phone system unless there is real business value being delivered. IP Telephony promises great value through the potential applications that one could develop and run on this Internet device. Most early adopters of IP Telephony are not sure yet what such applications might be. Their thinking is not made easier by the fact that this wonderful new Internet device looks like a phone and talks like a phone. Getting corporations to think beyond the phone is a challenge, so IP Telephony vendors furiously demonstrate capabilities such as tracking FedEx packages, looking up stock quotes, doing directory lookups and selectively screening or routing calls. These features in and of themselves seldom justify the cost of IP Telephony.

There are very creative applications of convergence solutions in real businesses. Voice activated access to prescription drug ingredients saves pharmacists time, and patient data on phones outside operating theaters increases accuracy of patient data capture and shortens billing cycles. How does one know whether one is investing in high-payback applications instead of just buying the latest technology? This is the subject of this chapter.

There was a faulty premise underlying much of the investment in the heyday of the Dot-com phenomenon: people confused infrastructure investments with investments in specific applications that enabled core business processes. The same is true when it comes to the second wave of Internet technologies such as mobile applications, storage area networks, voice activated Web-based applications and more. Why is it that we live in this perpetual confusion? It is, in part, because the speed of the Internet world in which we live makes us prone to believe in quick fixes and fragmented solutions, and we consider it too lofty a thing to systematically consider the end-to-end implications of technology and other trends.

Common questions on investments

CEO: *What will be the bottom line impact of investments in I-Operations?*

Most executive teams contain a mixture of people. Some believe increased revenues to be critical parts of their business plans, others advocate decreased operating costs. Some executives emphasize the potential for enhanced customer service. For others, facilitating the prospective cultural changes taking place could be the most pressing issue. Regardless of your issues, here are some strategies that will impact your success:

- Begin your I-Operations initiative with a clear statement of the impact that you want to have; then determine the level of investment required to achieve that desired impact.

- Assess the cost of not making the investments. I-Operations is not about some new-fangled thing you can either embrace or ignore. For major corporations, it is simply the price of being in business.

- There are two ways to improve the bottom line; increasing revenues is one of them. The Internet should open up new sales channels and, possibly, new markets for your corporation.
- Cost reductions are becoming more commonplace in the Internet Economy. There are new examples every week of internal processes becoming more efficient when Internet-enabled. Although the hype of the Internet economy has subsided, a silent revolution of relentless Internet-based cost reductions has continued.
- Perhaps the greatest bottom line impact in the future will come from extending your definition of the Operating Model to your ecosystem of partners through I-Operations. The costs of inefficiencies at the boundaries between organizations can be enormous. For example, a chip shortage at one supplier will ripple throughout related companies and industries. The ubiquitous nature of Internet technologies makes partnering a strategic imperative and an achievable reality.

CEO: *What cultural changes will I need to make?*
This is an interesting question. Elsewhere in this book we have dealt with the cultural aspects of the Internet Revolution. But the real questions CEOs are asking are about them, the CEO: "What do I have to do?" And, not usually stated, but often implied: "Am I up to it?" The answer to this question will depend in great measure on what type of leader you are. Simply put, if you are a command-and-control, hierarchical, and keep-things-centralized executive, then changes will be required. However, even if you are a more relaxed, employee-empowerment proponent who encourages discretionary initiatives, success is not guaranteed. In

answering the question, it may be helpful to examine five different types of leaders, then consider the cultural changes they may need to make.

The Institute has developed a model of leadership called LEMON Leadership™. The scope of this book does not include this analysis and psychology of leadership types and styles. However, at a rudimentary level, you may recognize yourself in the five leadership types and find helpful insights on your course of action. The model contains five types (as opposed to styles) of leaders who see things differently, hear and speak differently, and have a different definition of reality. Naturally, each type of leader will have different strengths, weaknesses and imperatives when it comes to I-Operations.

Type of Leader	Response to I-Operations
Luminary	(+) Readily accepts new things; jumps all over the Internet as the next thing. (-) Abandons core business. ("By next week we will be an e-business. Everything that is not e, is not.") Must: bring people along deliberately, with a practical path for the organization to follow.
Entrepreneur	(+) Seizes on new business/revenue opportunities. ("We have a great new revenue source.") (-) Doesn't think through required changes in core operations. Must: ensure that the Operating Model can be put in place, on time, to deliver on promises.
Manager	(+) Sees potential for cost reduction and structural change. ("Finally I have a vehicle for driving consistency throughout my

	organization, internationally, wherever anyone has a browser.") (-) Over-regulates the cultural side of Internet. ("...and you will all do it my way.") Must: be tight on processes, and looser on culture.
Organizer	(+) Likes Internet-speed. ("Now I can do things without being encumbered by the formal organization.") (-) Rushes into implementation before developing a cohesive I-Operations strategy. ("...hey, where's my back-up?") Must: deliberately explore the end-to-end implications of I-Operations, and avoid "just do it" philosophies.
Networker	(+) Sees the communication, partnering and networking potential of the Internet. Is a possibility thinker when it comes to new things. (-) Avoids the operational realities of what it takes to construct a comprehensive, Internet-enabled Operating Model. Must: discipline themselves to look beyond the "it all just happened" stories, and use their networking prowess to build a balanced team that will actually build things.

There is good news no matter what your leadership category. You do not fundamentally have to change your leadership DNA. But you do need to recognize your leadership type, because it will cause you to respond to emerging technologies in particular ways. Remember, leaders lead out of their identity, not their style. Who you are will determine your bias when it comes to your response to disruptive emerging technologies.

CEO: *How much time should my executive team spend on I-Operations?*

If you assign the right people to the right tasks and make the right investments, your executive team should be able to treat it as any other initiative. Status and exception reporting at the executive levels should suffice.

CEO: *Do I have to initiate I-Operations?*

No, but you do have to create the climate in which I-Operations can flourish, and while you don't have to—and probably won't—have the genius ideas, you should quickly develop a picture in your mind of how the Internet and its implementation by others in your organization will change the face and fiber of your corporation.

Next-level management: *How do we motivate our executives to make major investments in I-Operations?*

Have them read this book. (We apologize for sounding self-serving, but we believe in I-Operations.) Then use the tried and tested arguments you use for other initiatives:

- *Customers*: our customers say we have to do this in order to keep serving them.
- *Competition*: our competitors are getting ahead of us and it will cost us market share.
- *Costs*: other companies are reducing the costs of their operations with new technologies, and we are stuck in our old patterns.
- *Retention of employees*: we are losing key staff to corporations that are offering them personal growth opportunities.

Perhaps more compelling is to give them an up-close-and-personal look at what your company or others are accomplishing with the Internet. We know numerous executives who have never even looked at their own company's website.

Next-level management: *How do you budget for I-Operations?*

In a recent speech at Internet World, former Treasury Secretary Robert Rubin stated, "There has been, and still is, a belief held by too many that the so-called New Economy has repealed the laws of human nature and economics." But he noted that other society-shifting technological developments, such as the telephone and the automobile, still abided by the same economic rules that all other businesses followed—that is, companies had to quickly show profits in order to succeed.[22] There has been a more healthy recognition of Return on Investment (R.O.I.), but still not enough emphasis on exactly what will be done with the infrastructure. The "and then a miracle happens" mindset has not yet disappeared.

Our research indicates that investments in Information Technology have increased among those corporations who consider themselves to be leaders in I-Operations. Typically, the payback periods of New World Applications are measured in months, as opposed to years. Success with such applications will, therefore, spawn requests for more. If you are contemplating a major change in business workflow with correspondingly significant initial investments, embracing good fiscal management is, of course, the responsible thing to do. In this case, don't overdo frugality: we caution you to remember that I-Operations is a mandate, not a luxury.

Investment barriers to I-Operations

Expanding on these investment questions, research indicates that corporations fall into two major groups when it comes to investing in the Internet and related technologies. We have labeled them leaders and laggards. The graph indicates that they struggle with very different issues. Those who are opposed to Internet technologies have a higher incidence of trust and communication issues. Those who have deployed Internet technologies have progressed to the "back end/front end" integration issues. In other words, if a corporation is still asking the WHY questions (rather than the HOW, questions), they are probably a laggard.

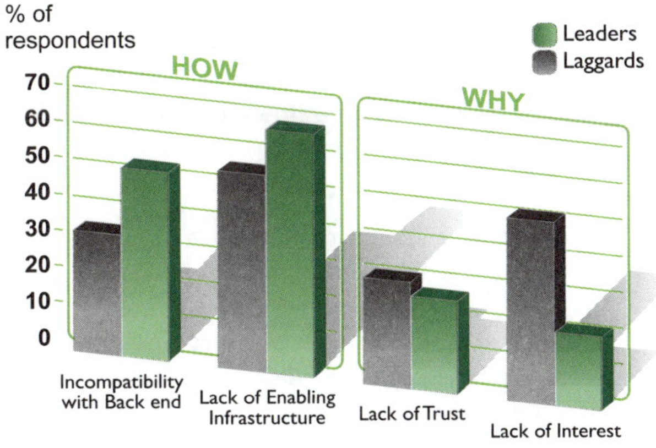

Perceived hindrances to I-Operations[23]

In our research we uncovered additional data about the major obstacles to I-Operations. Eighty percent of the executives interviewed stated that they believe legacy people are the greatest hindrance to developing I-Operations.

This statement received highest ratings among those interviewed: "Lack of vision is a significant hindrance to developing I-Operations." Only 40% indicated that legacy systems are a major hurdle.

Beyond the people or systems issues, we spoke with executives about other impediments to e-business. Lack of knowledge of Internet technologies was the fourth highest-ranking impediment, right behind the historic culture of corporations.

There were a number of items that ranked relatively low among the list of concerns around Internet investments:

- *Previous investment in old positioning*. Those corporations that recognize that the Internet is a fact of life do not seem interested in wasting time refuting it just to justify their former market positioning.

Old Thinking vs. Old Systems

As mentioned previously, legacy thinking is a bigger obstacle to overcome than legacy systems. Old ways of thinking are often deeply ingrained within management of traditional corporations.

Statement | **Survey Results**

The greatest inhibitor of product innovation is legacy systems.

The greatest inhibitor of product innovation is legacy people—old thinking.

- *Legacy systems.* Historically, some corporations have resisted new technologies (such as client-server or IP Telephony) on the basis that they have a large investment in legacy systems (such as mainframe computers or PBXs). We did not see much evidence of this type of thinking carrying over to Internet technologies.

- *Protection of past branding of products.* This also ranked low, possibly because forward-thinking marketers see the potential of the Internet to enhance features and brand products. If anything, for a period of time the pendulum swung the other way, and people carried the misconception that the Internet would enable them to build a brand if only they threw enough money at it, and sometimes regardless of whether they had an underlying product.

- *Lack of trained personnel.* While this was not a major obstacle, some executives expressed the concern that if they invested in training their employees, such employees would leave to go to other companies once they had been trained. This may be true, but if people are worth more after they have been trained, then perhaps they need to be paid more.

If you are still asking questions about what to do with the Internet, there is actually a more fundamental question to ask: "What is the Internet doing with you?" It is changing the way your staff thinks. It is connecting them to suppliers and customers in new ways. It is transforming the types of products you offer. It is extending your global corporate visibility. It is compressing cycle times, and raising your customers' expectations. By its very nature, it is not a technology in some corner of your organization. It is not the domain of some Dot-com spin-off that can be insulated from the rest of the corporation. It is not a single application, relegated to one department.

The Internet is changing your corporation, if only because it is changing your people, your customers and your competitors. Your job is to assign and re-assign corporate resources to ensure that every aspect of your Operating Model has been reconsidered in light of this suite of rapidly evolving, enabling technologies. If you as a corporate leader are unclear about the pervasiveness of I-Operations in your organization, we encourage your organization to take the I-Operations Assessment.

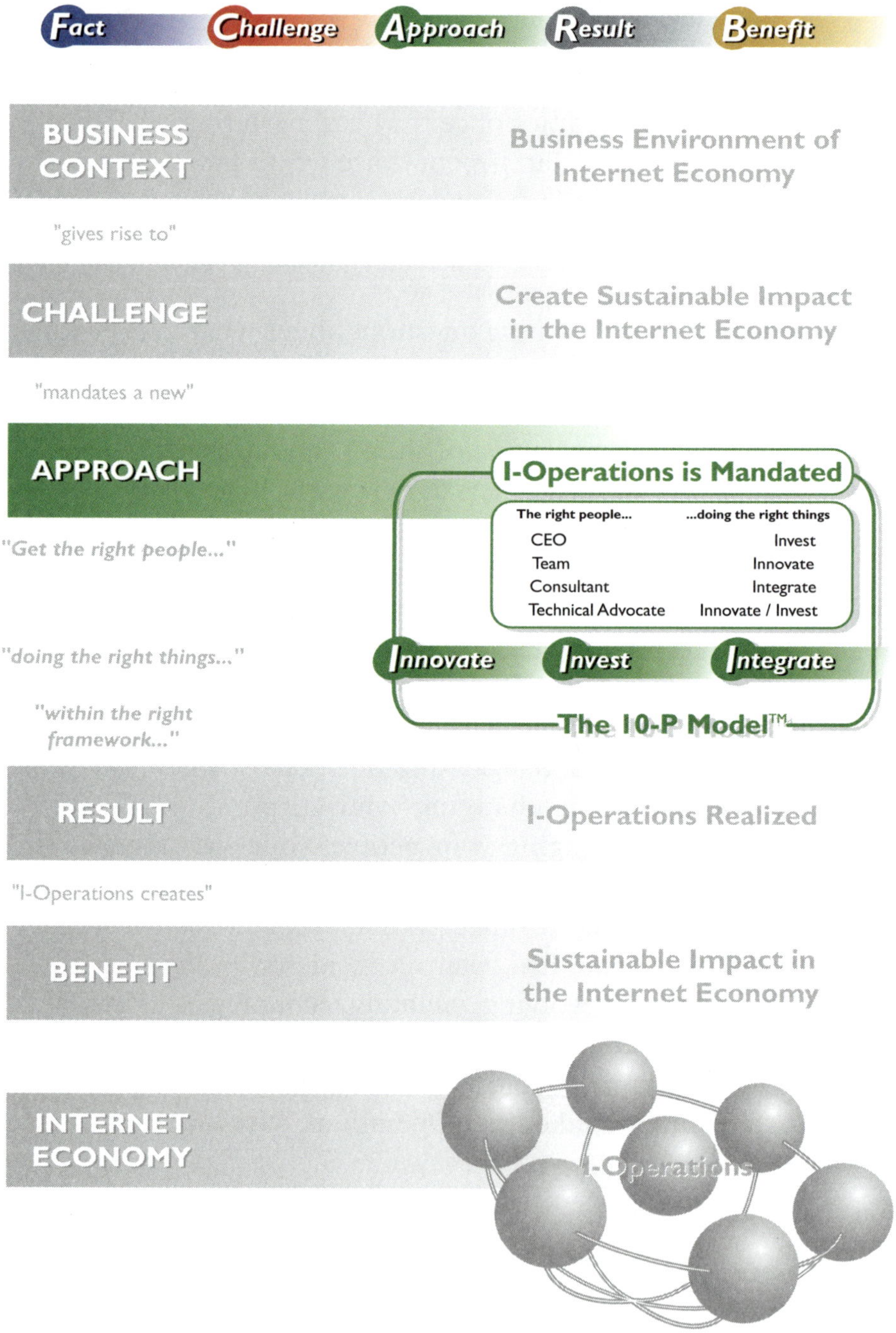
Fact
Challenge
Approach
Result
Benefit
BUSINESS CONTEXT
Business Environment of Internet Economy
"gives rise to"
CHALLENGE
Create Sustainable Impact in the Internet Economy
"mandates a new"
APPROACH
I-Operations is Mandated
The right people...
...doing the right things
CEO
Invest
Team
Innovate
Consultant
Integrate
Technical Advocate
Innovate / Invest
"Get the right people..."
"doing the right things..."
"within the right framework..."
Innovate
Invest
Integrate
The 10-P Model™
RESULT
I-Operations Realized
"I-Operations creates"
BENEFIT
Sustainable Impact in the Internet Economy
INTERNET ECONOMY
I-Operations

Chapter 7

I-Operations: Integration

Get the right people…

With the onslaught of challenges that are facing leaders at present—not the least of which is a flood of new technologies—it is telling that one of the most popular business books of recent years is *Who Moved My Cheese?*[24] which is hardly a cerebral or technical tome. This is consistent with our findings that the greatest obstacle to I-Operations is not legacy systems or the absence of technology, but legacy thinking, fear of change and the absence of leaders who are on a self-regimented e-business growth path.

On the positive side, our work revealed that senior executives play a key role in the adoption of Internet technologies and the implementation of Internet-enabled Operating Models. But they do not have to be the grand mastermind behind the ideas, or the technology expert, or the project manager for e-business.

Roles of key executives

A large percentage of surveyed executives indicated that the role of the CEO is to create the climate in which the Internet can take root in their corporation. Specifically this involves six tasks:

- *Advocate the Internet:* John Roth of Nortel Networks and his now famous "right turn" is a good example of advocacy.[25] Somewhat skeptical of the Internet, Roth went online to find a liner for the glove compartment of his Jaguar. The incident made him into an Internet advocate.
- *Believe:* Senior executives have to believe that the Internet is essential to the survival and transformation of their business. Skin-deep assent will not suffice.
- *Communicate:* The staff has to hear regularly and consistently from senior executives that e-business is business.
- *Delegate details:* Effective executives cast the vision and delegate the details, and they don't place their learning curve on the critical path.
- *e-Expenditures:* Retooling an end-to-end Operating Model to be Internet-enabled can be costly. But it is more costly to ignore it. Invest in infrastructure with specific business applications in mind.
- *Focus externally:* The CEO has to keep the organization pointed at the corporation's customers and external stakeholders.

To reiterate, the vast majority of Internet initiatives do not begin with the CEO. That role is left to others in the organization. The CEO must, however, create the environment for success.

A technical advocate almost always emerged from our surveys as having a specific role, namely that of proselytizing the use of Internet technologies in the operations of the business. A natural candidate for this position is the CIO. Over 30% of the time it is the CIO, and the remainder of the time it is another respected executive with the endorsement of the CIO. Most of the breakthrough ideas come from task forces, and not from the CIO or CEO. Very seldom are ideas formulated at the top and then pushed down through the organization. (Rare exceptions are where the CEO is also a luminary who routinely leads with his or her ideas.) Usually a purposeful "best of breed" internal task force is formed. It is quite common to find that outside consultants are hired to help assist in the implementation of the concepts.

One of the difficulties we experienced in conducting research of this nature was identifying one person with a solid grasp of the entire, end-to-end Operating Model. Chief Operating Officers (COO) are often the best candidates. Sometimes the CEO is this person, when the organization is still small and the corporation revolves around the insights of the CEO. But for the most part, we are reminded of Johnson's Law: "In every organization there is only one person who knows everything that's going on... and they should be fired." If the first part of this law is true for your organization, please do not deploy part two! Instead, we would advocate that all corporations consider embracing an individual or body of individuals who fully comprehend the Operating Model. It may be a tag-on to the job description of the COO or a function reporting to him or her. But the vision and knowledge of the Operating Model, including the end-to-end processes and cultural practices across the corporation and its partners, should exist somewhere at the senior level of an organization.

Cisco's own experience closely reflects what the research determined as the successful course of action. The roles and responsibilities of their executives align with those executives in other I-Operations companies. Senior executives possess a strong body of knowledge of the Operating Model. Subsets of this model are clearly understood within the functional lines of business, finance, sales, marketing and distribution.

The CEO of Cisco has molded the environment, and even mandated that New World Applications be incubated and deployed. Regular meetings with mandatory senior executive attendance and accountability are held to review progress. The CIO and his team consistently proselytize the use of Internet technologies for opportunities in the Internet Economy.

Most ideas have percolated from cross-functional teams comprised of outstanding performers. Subsequently, the applications are deployed by the same (or similar) team of experts, and almost every major New World Application has been deployed with the assistance of an external consultant.

Customer support is a superb example of a New World Application being designed and deployed in this manner at Cisco. A small team of I.T. and customer support personnel wanted to deliver a higher level of client satisfaction at a lower level of expenditures. Conventional (and non-Internet) thinking dictates that technology vendors increase the number of field support personnel proportionately as their number of clients and business volumes increase. Not doing so would surely decrease client satisfaction and eventually revenues. Instead, this team developed a client support system that handles 80% of support requests without human intervention. This application resulted in annual savings of $506 million in fiscal year 2000, pushed directly through to the bottom line. Customer satisfaction—measured on a scale of 1 to 5—increased from 4.06 to 4.33 since Cisco implemented online customer support.[26] It seems logical to conclude that most clients would prefer expedited electronic answers and solutions rather than a human interface with its slower results.

The research shows that successful I-Operations companies bring the right people into the right roles. The CEO, CIO, cross-functional teams and consultants are the

Technology Advocate

One of our key observations of companies that had successfully integrated an Internet-enabled Operating Model was that they had a high-level technology advocate. For the purposes of this book, it is not our intention to suggest whom that person should be specifically, but that there is one. Our quantitative research showed that I-Operations companies had a much higher likelihood of having a high-level technology advocate leading the technology integration and implementation.

Statement	Survey Results: Leaders	Survey Results: Average
Is there a high-level technology advocate within your organization?	87%	70%
• CIO	31%	21%
• Executive-level	12%	17%
• CEO/President	18%	17%
• Board-level	15%	13%
• CFO	10%	11%
• VP-level	11%	10%
• COO	7%	5%

key players in partnership with senior management. The lead operating executive must clearly understand the Operating Model, with or without the Internet. Also, the appropriate functional executives must understand the Operating Model's functional subsets.

Doing the right things...

The Internet has fueled innovation. But innovation on its own is not enough. Many Dot-com companies proved that great technology is ineffective unless there is alignment of the core of the organization behind a focused purpose. Corporations must determine their desired impact up front. In this book, we seek to address the challenge of determining how to have sustainable impact in the Internet Economy. The Internet creates new opportunities for the creation of impact. It also mandates that we discover new ways in which to have impact. Many corporations can have temporary impact, and in the Internet Economy many organizations come and go very quickly.

Impact *Innovate* *Invest* *Integrate*

We have not seen the end of the failures in the Internet space; there will be many more in the years ahead, but the rate of technological and business change forces all corporations to revisit the question of impact frequently. We assume that if you have read this far, you are already convinced that your future impact is linked in some way to the Internet.

Many brick and mortar companies have been forced to reevaluate the Internet's effect on their impact. The grocery industry is one example. In the mid-1990s, Peapod developed an online grocery business. The major players considered their options, but essentially stayed on the sidelines (apart from relatively minor partnering excursions with Peapod). Then Webvan appeared with their much-touted IPO of $375 million.[27] Their website was better, they were well capitalized, and they lent credibility to online grocery shopping as a viable industry. Still, the major grocers stayed on the sidelines. Next, Webvan began to develop the brick and mortar infrastructure of a traditional grocer. They skipped the retail store phase, but they contracted with Bechtel for the construction of distribution centers. Then Albertsons and Safeway entered the e-tail space, leveraging their traditional assets. First, they leveraged their stores for pick-up/delivery. Second, they leveraged their I.T. infrastructure. Third, some grocery retailers leveraged the knowledge they had gained over many years about the buying patterns of customers, and, perhaps most importantly, they leveraged the confidence that customers have in them as a brand. Does this afford traditional grocers a more efficient use of assets than an online grocery business like Webvan? Since the first edition of this book, the bell has tolled for Webvan. It is a stark reminder that success in eight of the Ten Ps is not enough. Place (from distribution center to doorstep) and Profit were never properly reconciled or aligned or integrated. The legacy of Webvan may be that no major retail grocery chain can afford to ignore the Internet and Internet-enabled Operating Models as they consider what impact they want to have. That impact might be eliminating trips to the store, making trips quicker and more productive, or targeting products and prices to individual customers based on past shopping patterns.

Successful corporations take three steps to create sustainable impact in the Internet Economy.

They *Innovate*.

> Successful corporations are constantly looking for ways to make small and large changes in all aspects of their business. We have already dispelled the myth that such improvements need only be made in the single area where you believe your competitive advantage lies. To stay in the game, you have to improve on all fronts, at all times. Therefore, you have to innovate. Remember, innovations of infrastructure that do not lead to innovations in real business applications are not innovations at all. They are simply expenditures.

They make the right *Investments*.

This is different from throwing money at a problem. Too many corporations come up with brilliant ideas, and then rush headlong into a detailed implementation phase without really considering its cost. They fail to think through the real investments that are needed to accomplish their goals. Successful corporations do not just scratch the surface when it comes to investments in I-Operations. Successful organizations are realistic about R.O.I. Attempting to build a business case for enabling technologies without exploring the new ways of doing business that such technology enables is futile.

They *Integrate* the solution throughout the organization.

Integration goes beyond the traditional "systems integration" of implementing a complex suite of software applications. Integration has more to do with instituting an end-to-end set of processes, organizations/people, measurement systems, and enabling technologies that are fully aligned with the corporation's purpose and which deliberately deliver on its value proposition.

Think of the Operating Model as a 10-vertebrae spinal column of the organization. The organization functions best when the vertebrae are all aligned. To take the analogy further, Internet-enabled communications are the nerves. Communications to and from the extremities is better when all aspects of the Operating Model are aligned. When the profit models or sales incentives are out of line with marketing promotions, the results of the whole corporation suffer. When the behaviors of one department are inconsistent with the values of the corporation, the company loses money and reduces its impact. Successful corporations are integrated organizations. The Internet has the potential to take Integration to a whole new level, and tap the power of alignment.

Within the right framework...

We are living in a networked world, and our mental maps must reflect the fluidity and completeness that this implies. We must revisit the business models we learned in Business School and rethink what the Internet is doing to business. The new world mandates that we examine each of the 10-P Drivers of Impact for each of the steps that takes us towards Impact (Innovate, Invest, Integrate).

We will explore each of these in turn.

Innovate

Impact Innovate Invest Integrate

Not so long ago, Japanese companies would gather workers on the factory floors in the morning and have a corporate-sponsored chuckle. The company was supposed to reap all sorts of benefits from the group guffaw: productivity, employee joy, stress reduction... you name it. Mandating innovation will be about as effective as mandating laughter.

That said, the Internet carries with it a greater propensity to innovate. This has much to do with the communications and cultural changes fostered by Internet technologies. In the recent past a manager was distinguished from a worker by the manager's inside track on information. The "real information" flowed through an organization from the top to the bottom. Today, the

Internet makes huge quantities of information available to the person in the cube, and the knowledge worker has more time available to troll for information than does the manager. So the likelihood that the good ideas will flow from the top is dwindling. As time goes by, the notions of top and bottom will become less important than the "informed" vs. "uninformed" categories.

Innovation is often focused on products or services. This is a good place to start, but it is not where innovation should end. We advocate looking at every aspect of the Operating Model to come up with the potential for breakthrough ideas. Here are some questions to consider that we have abstracted from our survey:

Driver of Impact	***Innovation Questions to Consider***
Purpose	Mission Aviation Fellowship discovered a hidden asset in its communication networks. *What assets do we have—really—that could broaden/focus our purpose in the Internet Economy?*
Products	Apple's iPod puts a slice of the Internet in your pocket. *How can we develop products that are Internet-centric?*
Presence	Converged Communications allows customers to choose the medium that they prefer for customer service at many companies. *What would a corporate identity that integrates our legacy and Internet identities look like for our corporation?*
Positioning	Tommy Bahama invented a story, then built a brand. *Can the Internet enable us to reposition ourselves in old markets?*

Partnering	Leading software developers cross geographic, cultural and time zone barriers to collaborate in product development. *Can we remove process inefficiencies at the boundaries between our company and other corporations?*
Process	Oracle.com has dramatically enhanced its direct marketing and selling capability. *What are the innovation opportunities inherent in all our processes becoming customer facing?*
Place	Disney leverages theme parks, retail stores and online media to create impact. *How can we best leverage bricks and mortar without being encumbered by old thinking?*
People	Internet-enabled Converged Communications open new doors for collaboration through voice and video conferencing and services such as WebEx and Placeware. *What opportunities are there to radically transform our corporate culture?*
Planning	IP Telephones can collect information from employees rapidly. *How can we use the immediate response element of this Internet device to hardwire employee input into our planning?*
Profit	Oracle claims to have reduced expenses by $1 billion thanks to the Internet.

What cost-saving opportunities exist in each aspect of our Operating Model if we creatively use Internet technologies?

Invest

Many corporations have struggled to answer the question of how much to invest in Internet technologies. Behind this struggle lies a difficulty in figuring out what effect the Internet technologies have on the corporation's impact. We have already outlined the types of investments that need to be made in order to achieve I-Operations, but what are the guidelines that one should follow in deciding where, when and how much to invest?

Using Internet technologies to communicate with stakeholders

It is evident that lines of communication within and between organizations are clearer where organizations have implemented an Internet-enabled Operating Model.

Statement | **Survey Results**

Senior executives are more in touch with constituents using Internet technologies.

Internet/network-based communications have improved our interaction with customers.

Internet/network-based communications have enabled clearer lines of communication between divisions of the company.

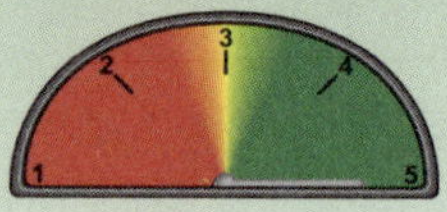

Employees have the ability to easily communicate with executives.

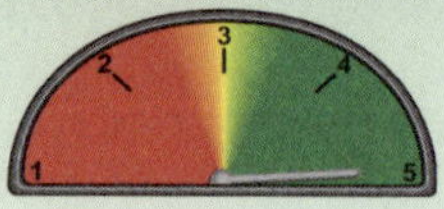

Investment in infrastructure often precedes any New World Application deployment. Although this statement is obvious, its profound implications should not be lost. Without technology, there are no New World Application deployments; there are no New World Application ideas. Conscious decisions have been made to invest in New World Applications at Cisco, with tremendous paybacks. The infrastructure is the prerequisite for the application and is part of the up-front expenditure. In other words, they have reasons for, and even a philosophy of, technology investments. Yet technology investments for the sake of technology alone are not made.

Impact Innovate **Invest** Integrate

As we stated earlier, it is critical to buy the technology and build the infrastructure. This must be done under the philosophy that the follow-on New World Applications will be deployed because they are mandates for your company and your industry. The projected business impact of these applications should determine your appropriate investment level. This chicken and egg dilemma can be overcome by using a predictable approach to uncovering high payback applications for emerging technologies. If you are waiting for the full maturation of your application idea prior to making any infrastructure investment, you are losing valuable time—time that may be to your competitors' advantage. And if you simply buy technology and hope that the applications will materialize, you will be disappointed. As a practical matter, you may wish to build an emerging technologies laboratory in which new applications for emerging technologies can be explored by business users in a controlled environment.

Integrate

The final component of "doing the right thing within the right framework" is Integration. We have defined Integration as "a state of collaboration between and alignment among all aspects of the Operating Model, toward the end of producing maximized impact." The deployment of an Internet-enabled Operating Model is different for every corporation. Throughout the implementation, there should always be a line of sight back to the purpose (and core business) of the corporation. Technology has a way of clouding the thinking of those who would otherwise make clear judgments. When planning the set of detailed projects and tasks that make up the integration plan, it is, therefore, important to consider a set of questions that will help ensure that the implementation is focused on the right elements.

Impact Innovate Invest **Integrate**

Driver of Impact	***Integration questions to consider***
Purpose	Jack Welch mandated a two year transition to e-business for GE. *What steps can the CEO take to provide the climate in which an I-Operations implementation will best succeed?*
Products	Avaya has charted a course that blends traditional PBX with Voice over IP (VoIP). *How can we redesign our Product Architecture to integrate Internet and other products in the same framework?*
Presence	Schwab scrapped e-Schwab in favor of an integrated identity. *How can we ensure that our online*

	presence and "offline" presence are consistently aligned?
Positioning	Many e-tailers made promises, but they did not deliver. *What must we do to ensure that any external positioning is completely aligned with internal realities?*
Partnering	Lucent has account teams that share deal information across continents. *What is the best design and development strategy for our ecosystem/Impact Network?*
Process	Many companies use the Internet to front end their back office systems. *How do we overcome any lack of integration between our own front end and back office systems?*
Place	Bookstores, coffee shops and Internet cafés readily blend the physical and virtual worlds. *How do we open new channels to interact with clients, customers, partners, and suppliers? How do the "bricks and clicks" analogies apply to our corporation?*
People	Cultural changes fueled by technology changes are leading to more and more "networked organizations" (not just technically, but from an organizational design perspective). *How do we shape our organization to best deliver our e-business value proposition? How do we provide access to information and decision authority internally and externally?*
Planning	A corporation solicits input from its customers using a Web-based tool prior to starting its annual planning.

	How do we open up the limitations on who plans? How will we plan for "e" throughout the Operating Model (end-to-end)?
Profit	Cisco has excellent productivity per employee. *What new Key Performance Indicators will we need to measure I-Operations?*

There is a second aspect of Integration that goes beyond the mechanics of project management and technology implementation. It is not uncommon to find that corporations do not realize their full potential, because major areas are not aligned. The premise behind the 10-P Model is that every spoke of the wheel requires a different level of investment, staffing and enabling technology. Each corporation has to figure out the right mixture of elements that, when combined together in a cohesive framework, produces the targeted impact. The strength of The 10-P Model is that it provides a framework for corporations to systematically consider all of the key variables at once.

Look back at past initiatives in your corporation. If the company has existed for 10 to 20 years, you would have seen your fair share of the latest thing. You probably remember Value Chain Analysis, Total Quality Management (TQM), *In Search of Excellence*, Shareholder Value Creation, Business Process Redesign (BPR), *Reinventing Competition*, *The Death of Competition*, *Reengineering Management*, Change Management and Organizational Transformation, *Crossing the Chasm* and so on. We won't mention all the waves of enabling technologies that accompanied such management initiatives. The question is, what makes I-Operations different? Is it the enabling technologies? They certainly open up new Innovation and Impact possibilities, not to mention Investment. Or were these past initiatives too narrowly focused on one or two spokes of the wheel? We believe the latter to be the case.

We also believe that looking at the complete Operating Model, end-to-end, and deliberately addressing every aspect in one coherent framework is a key differentiator. We are not advocating one particular technology, one special spoke, or one magical measure. Sustained impact dictates an integrated, cohesive look at your corporation. In a world of Internet speed, incredible competition, and heightened visibility of all stakeholders, including competitors, you cannot afford to say that you will address the integration aspects later, or you will get to investment in people later, or you will figure out the economic model later.

Today, alignment means a silver thread through the Four I's and a plumb line down The 10-Ps. Does this take too much time? Hardly. Our research shows that having the intellectual framework in place dramatically shortens the visioning/strategy cycle, and frees up resources to invest and integrate. What happens when technology changes? This is a timeless framework, so simply run through the cycle again and consider the fresh opportunities afforded by the new technology. This leads to real results.

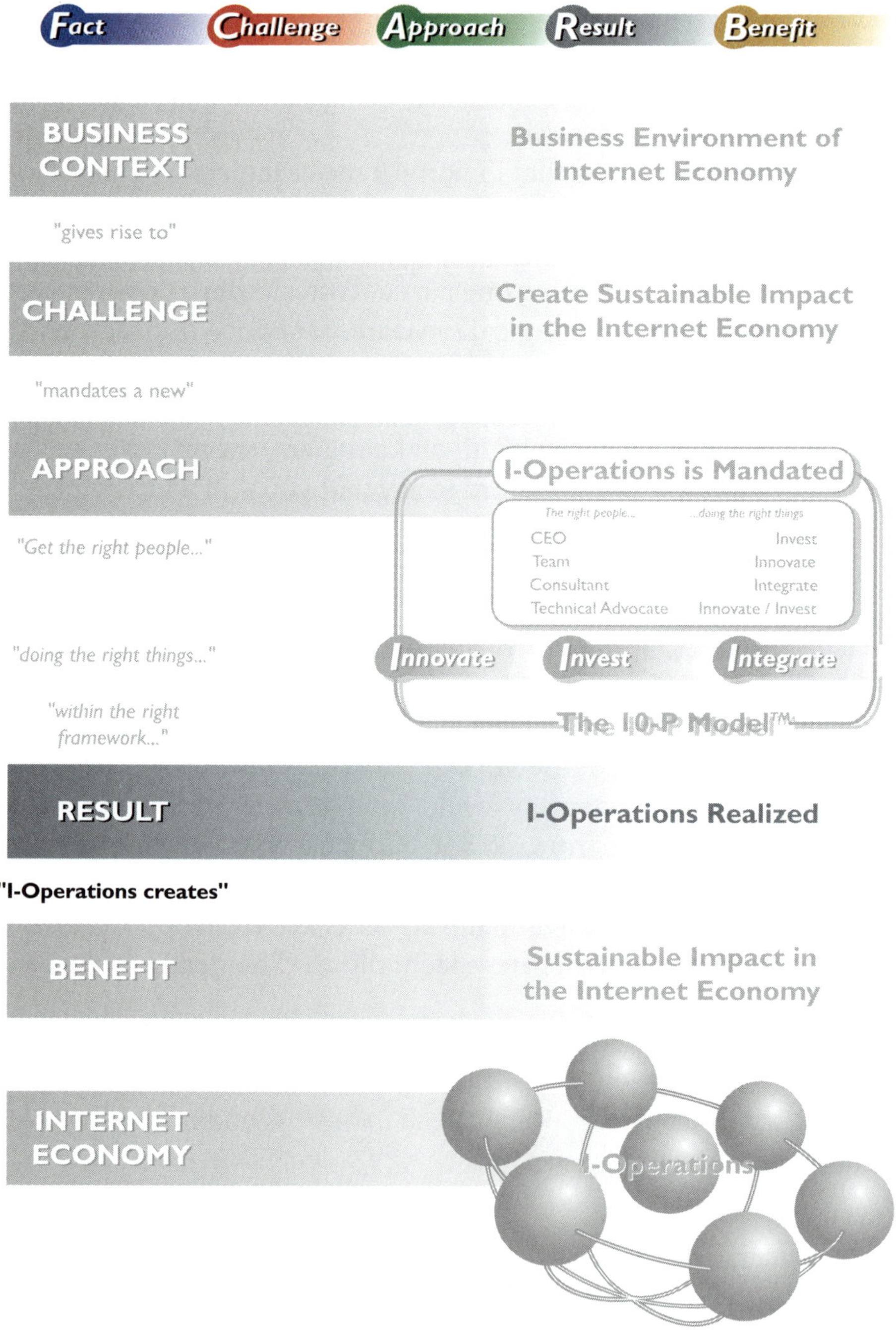
Fact
Challenge
Approach
Result
Benefit
BUSINESS CONTEXT
Business Environment of Internet Economy
"gives rise to"
CHALLENGE
Create Sustainable Impact in the Internet Economy
"mandates a new"
APPROACH
I-Operations is Mandated
The right people...
...doing the right things
CEO
Invest
Team
Innovate
Consultant
Integrate
Technical Advocate
Innovate / Invest
"Get the right people..."
"doing the right things..."
Innovate
Invest
Integrate
"within the right framework..."
The I0-P Model™
RESULT
I-Operations Realized
"I-Operations creates"
BENEFIT
Sustainable Impact in the Internet Economy
INTERNET ECONOMY
I-Operations

Chapter 8

Result

I-Operations: Realized

By now you will have noted that this publication is not a technical treatise on the Internet, nor an attempt to create a compendium of best practices in business. It is, however, an appeal to executives to have an end-to-end strategy for their Operating Model. It should be of particular benefit to that person in the corporation who carries the mantle of the Chief "e2e" Officer. Often this is the Chief Operating Officer, but in reality, people with a variety of titles can have this role. Realizing I-Operations requires practical strategies that will depend on your corporation's type. We have tailored our recommendations to five groups: Brick and Mortar, Born Wired, Pure Internet Plays, Philanthropic Organizations, and Academia.

Brick and Mortar

One of the first challenges that brick and mortar companies will have to address is leadership. "Good leaders are constantly acquiring tools; weak leaders have grown content with their tools."[28] On the leadership front, we recommend an approach that includes these steps:

- Acquire the necessary leadership tools to function in the Internet Economy.

- Assemble an e-team that includes representatives who have never experienced the Old Economy.
- Set deadlines for becoming an e-business. Jack Welch at GE did this well.
- Become more available to your people—the ones with the e-ideas—via e-mail and other electronic media. Dismantle traditional access barriers that came with brick and mortar.

> **"You have to undo strong beliefs to implement Internet Operations in old companies with old management."**
> *Pete Mountanos*[29]

- Recognize that your leadership decisions are becoming more and more transparent. Markets and employees respond almost immediately to major leadership actions.

Beyond the leadership opportunities, take an inventory of your real assets. The Internet can cause structural changes in industries, which may significantly alter value propositions. An amalgamation of trends can also shift the real value of your organization from one part of your portfolio to another. Take a fresh look at your real assets, but don't blindly abandon the assets that brought you to your present position. The "bricks and clicks" or "clicks and mortar" strategies are a blending of Old and Internet Economy assets. As you create new strategies, consider the following:

- *Confirm your core business; know what it is.* Now envision it as an e-Business. If you are a major player in your industry, think through your role in the Internet Economy. "Internet strategy is really business strategy. People who are focused on Internet strategy for its own sake are that way because they don't have business strategy."[30]

- *Rethink vertical integration.* Bandwidth and infrastructure breakthroughs obviate the need for vertical integration. While the cultural aspects of partnering are still challenging, partnering is far more practical today than it has ever been because of Internet technologies.

- *Partner like never before.* The opportunities for blurring the boundaries between corporations are greater than ever before. Business process redesign removed the vertical stovepipes within organizations through the enabling technology of relational databases. EDI has existed for many years, but costs and complexity prevented widespread use. The ease of use and pervasiveness of Web-enabled applications provide a context that allows one to rethink the boundaries of the corporation. Relatively few companies are deliberately integrating their Operating Models with those of partners, but the whole ASP push is the beginning of that wave.

> **"[Schwab] had created a separate e-business called e.Schwab, but about two years ago they realized it was the wrong thing to do because it made customers choose between Schwab and e.Schwab."[31]**
> *FORTUNE November 8*

- *Be deliberate about how you "incubate" an e-business within your corporation.* The Charles Schwab Corporation started a separate business and then had to integrate it with its original business. This experience is a lesson in both value propositions and Operating Models. If your customers are looking for an integrated product, be cautious about segmenting your Operating Model. Barnes & Noble is another example of a company that seemed confused on

> **"There's only one thing harder than starting a dot.com business: starting a dot.com within a traditional business."[32]**
> *Chris Yates, CTO, EA.com*

this issue and also did not recognize what its real assets were. It separated its e-business from its brick and mortar stores, and lost opportunities to leverage the brand it had built. Toyota looked for someone who could "break the rules while keeping our business goals and strategy in mind."[33] While their electronic commerce strategy team was not aimed at starting a new business, they became a catalyst for cultural change and e-strategy.

- *Re-create your culture.* Before the Internet really took off, society was reinventing itself every three to five years. Executives we spoke with often talked about gaining four years experience in one year. How often is your corporate culture being refreshed? Below the cute cultural trimmings such as free lunch, logo-laden car wraps and bring-your-dog-to-work days, lies a real cultural phenomenon that is as much generational/societal as it is technological (if one can separate these elements). While the post-Dot-com economic downturn has trued the reality index of many people, it has not reversed the cultural changes. A plummeting NASDAQ should not be seen as a signal to return to the downsides of old ways. Likewise, a soaring stock market should not be a license to suspend reality. Understand culture, and incorporate what supports your core purpose.

- *Do not abandon your core values, but deliberately rethink their implications in today's world.* Values generally remain stable; the implications of values can deteriorate if not reconsidered fairly frequently. The Internet increases the speed at which corporate values appear worn.

Born wired

Cisco Systems is often cited as an example of a company that has harnessed Internet-type technologies to become a major player in the Internet Economy. While this is true, the executives of legacy business correctly pointed out that corporations such as Cisco and Sun might not be the best examples of how to move from the Old to the Internet Economy. They have always been wired—even if their founding pre-dates the Internet phenomenon of late. This was borne out in an interview with executives at a major computer corporation in Silicon Valley. We started by asking, "What's changed in your business since the Internet?" They replied, "Nothing." As we reflected on this we recognized that they, too, were born wired.

I-Operations Myths

- ✓ You have to be a high-tech company to have I-Operations
- ✓ Only start-ups have I-Operations
- ✓ An I-Culture (part of I-Operations) automatically comes with Internet technology
- ✓ I-Operations is primarily the concern of your I.T. division
- ✓ Having a website presence = I-Operations
- ✓ E-Commerce = I-Operations
- ✓ I-Operations can't be implemented in large companies with traditional business models
- ✓ Our company is not an Internet business
- ✓ If it ain't broke, don't change it—we can continue to operate as we have in the past
- ✓ Our industry will not be affected by the Internet hype

Further dialogue revealed that those corporations who classify themselves as always-been-wired can still take these important steps forward:

- *Find the untouched pockets in your organization.* As is typical in many corporations, you probably have fabulous Web-enabled customer service applications, but the process you used to develop them took endless meetings and hundreds—if not thousands—of hours revising Microsoft Project plans. Is your product development Web-enabled? What is your meeting-to-decision ratio? And how long does it take a supplier to get through the "approved vendor" maze at your organization? Generally accepted practices have generally not been I-vamped yet. Find the untouched pockets.

- *Keep a steep learning curve in your organization.* Arrogance kills, partly because arrogant companies stop learning.
- *Move from egocentric to principled leadership.* The Internet has uncovered—if not created—some wonderful leadership talent, but you must not let raw talent and enthusiastic intuition forever blind you to the disciplines of principled management.
- *Listen to your customers.* Really. Remember that you have never had the experience of starting unwired.

Pure Internet plays

Not so long ago it was totally cool to tell your friends, "We're a pure Internet play," but that was in the days when the market had more froth than Starbucks, and part of the de-frothing was a quick renaming to ASP, B2B, P2P, wireless, or infrastructure something or other.

But the questions remain. What is your purpose? What is the essence of your business? What's your value proposition? How is your Operating Model lined up to fully support your offering? And, what is your economic model, the one that leads to profitability, not just thousands of "customers"?

More Myths
for the
Pure Net Players

- ✓ **Building a Website is easy**
- ✓ **Traffic will make you rich**
- ✓ **Smart money makes you smart**
- ✓ **Razzle-dazzle makes Websites great**
- ✓ **Brand is everything**
- ✓ **Wild ads make web stars**
- ✓ **Community, community**

Source: Inc. Magazine

The Internet daily challenges the fundamentals of the Old Economy. For example, thanks to Napster, copyright laws written in 1909 were challenged because someone broke the mold. Yet not everything that happened before the Internet was bad.

RedEnvelope.com is a good example of a company that appeared to be a pure Internet play but planned to expand to other channels at the appropriate time. In an interview, Tom Bazonne clearly articulated his strategy as being a blend of Internet, catalogue, and retail channels. His focus is on managing a brand across multiple channels, not just optimizing an Internet play.

The cumulative wisdom that comes from what we learned in our interviews and personal business experience suggests the following "back to basics" path for Internet players:

- Sharpen your purpose.
- Don't expand your product line just because the Internet makes it easy to do so.
- Understand the experience your customers desire, and make it happen for them on your website.
- Aggressively use technology to remove costs from your supply chain.
- Where you suspect you may have even marginal inefficiencies or sub-par competencies, find a partner.
- Instill discipline without becoming a dinosaur.
- Measure, measure, measure. The Peter Drucker quote, "What's measured, improves," is no less true for the Internet. In fact, we have better monitoring and measurement tools than ever before. Then make sure you measure the right things. Pete Mountanos says, "Non-Internet-enabled companies usually don't have the measurement systems in

place to allow them to see the hidden costs."[34] While Internet companies have the technical leg-up in measurement, brick and mortar companies have more experience in measuring hard facts.

Philanthropic organizations

Innovation in philanthropic organizations has mostly occurred at the customer-facing end of their businesses. Many charities have been inventive in pushing the edge, using available technologies to reach their target audiences. Since the middle of the last century, Mission Aviation Fellowship (MAF) had used its fleet of small airplanes to fly missionaries into remote locations. By the 1990s there were chartered airlines operating in many of the formerly remote locations. So MAF reevaluated their assets and discovered that they had a new one in their communications infrastructure. By 1995 they had added communications to their charter: "Telecommunications servicing 32 countries: electronic mail, electronic conferencing, website hosting, satellite phones and HF/VHF radio."[35] At the other end of the spectrum, we recently saw a Psion hand-held computer linked to a communications device which transmits e-mail twice a day between a satellite and anywhere on Earth. It was developed by a handful of volunteers, using basic materials. For about $40 a month, you never have to be unconnected. While more expensive than AOL or Juno, this solution is designed for remote users... very remote. Yet another advance has been in the use of DVD devices to communicate with illiterate people—high technology with a low-tech application.

Most of these creative uses of technology have been applied only in the field, however, and the Operating Model of many non-profits remains untouched by the Internet. The surface reason for this appears to be thriftiness, but is really philosophical. A penny saved on infrastructure is an extra penny for the field. This was laudable in the old days, but with the vanishing front end/back office distinctions, this dualistic (or dichotomized) thinking is harmful. The more subtle aspect is the fact that many organizations place more value on front-line workers than on those running the infrastructure. If technology investments are made with a line of sight to end customers, however, then such investments in enabling technologies can indeed have a direct impact on the accomplishment of the non-profit's mission. And with all aspects of the Operating Model becoming stakeholder-facing, all people in the organization and all systems become stakeholder-facing, and there is no longer a need for second class systems or people.

A second reason why some non-profits have only used technology in the field is their reluctance to tackle the rejuvenation of their Operating Models. A number of non-profits are run by original founders in their sunset years, who have had a lasting imprint on the modus operandi of their organizations. Perhaps we will see major changes in Operating Models that coincide with leadership transition of these established charities. Where we do see changes coming, the first movers are not traditional charities.

In our dealings with clients, we have seen the early signs of how I-Operations is beginning to revolutionize the world of philanthropy. It is hard to tell whether there is one single driver of this fundamental change, because there appear to be at least four phenomena occurring simultaneously.

Wealth transfer

We are standing at the brink of the greatest inter-generational wealth transfer in history. Conservative estimates show that $10 trillion is about to change hands.

Other estimates show that the number could be $40 trillion to $170 trillion.[36] Those involved in running foundations know that the current channels of giving are totally inadequate to handle this coming surge. For most charities, additional income means adding staff on a proportional basis to process grant requests and disburse funds.

This wealth transfer problem is exacerbated by the fact that more wealth has been generated in the last ten years than at any other decade in history. There is a new set of "mega donors" emerging. One big splash came from Ted Turner with his $1 billion pledge and another from the Bill and Melinda Gates Foundation. Venture Philanthropists have been attempting to transfer the Venture Capitalist principles to charitable giving. There have even been high-tech investment funds created in Silicon Valley where approved investors have a social obligation to donate some of their gains to charity. Yet others have started business incubators where participating entrepreneurs are required to set aside some of their pre-IPO stock or a percentage of profits for charitable contributions. While we recognize that more is said than actually done when it comes to philanthropy, these are all still real examples of why the present philanthropic infrastructure will feel like a grass snake trying to swallow a sheep.

Supply-line seepage

People are waking up to the vast inefficiencies in the way donors are relieved of their money. It is not uncommon for the fund-raising budgets of charities to be 15% to 25% or more of every dollar donated. Most of this is collected through mail solicitations with the traditional 0.3% response rates, and the rest comes from "large donor management" activities. The system is inefficient.

For more mechanized giving, such as monthly United Way contributions, the administrative portion is still typically 10¢ to 15¢ on the dollar, primarily because the collection efforts are mostly still manual. In addition, companies usually spend another 5¢ supporting United Way efforts. Enter the Internet. With a fully Web-enabled infrastructure, early entrants are claiming to get the job done for less than three to five cents for every dollar donated thereby reducing costs for both the company and United Way. For most organizations, however, seepage remains a big problem.

To illustrate the point, donors pledged $12.5 billion to foreign missions in 2000. Of that, only $3.5 billion will actually be given, and only 7.5% of the $12.5 billion pledged will actually reach the field.[37] That's seepage. A more recent example is the Red Cross's diversion of donations earmarked for September 11 victims, not to mention those telemarketers who retain 94% of money extracted from donors.

Business as philanthropy

A third dimension to the gradual transformation of philanthropic organizations is a smaller, but rapidly growing, group of leaders who aim to "do well while doing good." They are deploying the disciplines, legal structure and Operating Models of for-profit businesses to do the work that would formerly have been done by non-profits. They are effectively creating self-funding ministry models.

The Institute is currently working with companies who have set up Web-enabled models to handle end-to-end operations for churches, specialized accounting for tax-exempt organizations, and free online estate planning for donors who are considering leaving money to their favorite charity (rather then Uncle Sam).

Changed customers

Forward-thinking charities have awakened to the reality that the Internet is transforming the thinking or worldview of the people they are trying to serve. If the charities plan to identify and meet the needs of these customers, then they have to quickly understand them. Saddleback Community Church provides streaming video of church services, intranet sites for departments, e-mail accounts with filtering for objectionable content, and much more. Its church campus is wired with fiberoptic cable, and it has an I.T. staff of 12 people led by a former Microsoft employee. About 160 technically qualified volunteers support the full-time staff. They have ancillary websites for pastors (pastors.com) and for those participating in their "Purpose Driven" programs (PurposeDriven.com), to name a few. Why go to this length? They do it to accomplish their vision and reach the people in their sphere of influence. Who are these people? Many of them appear to be technically savvy: 40% of the church-goers enjoy high-speed Internet access. Those without a computer can sign up and take advantage of Saddleback's bulk purchasing arrangements with a computer supplier.

Challenges

Despite these four big changes and the isolated examples, few philanthropic agencies deploy I-Operations throughout their organization. Why is this? There are numerous challenges for leaders of charities who wish to pursue integrated I-Operations:

> **"In today's challenging global economy, companies can do well by reining in expenses and focusing on profits. They can also succeed by building, maintaining, and growing their commitment to corporate giving programs. If managed well, corporate philanthropy can be an integral part of a company's strategy, regardless of the state of the economy."**
>
> John Morgridge
> Chairman, Cisco Systems, Inc.

- *Understand how the Internet is changing your target audience/customer.* As the Mahatma Gandhi is reported to have said, "I must go now, for there go my people and I am their leader." The Internet will provide increased access to donors, but these donors are of a generation that demand increased accountability and visibility of results.

- *Embrace change.* The Internet demands new thinking and rapid adjustments. Systemic thinking that incorporates networked structures is essential, albeit bewildering, to leaders and participants. Change is meant to be disruptive. Avoiding inevitable change is even more disruptive.

- *Rethink resources.* Many non-profits tackle major change initiatives using volunteers who are well meaning, but unqualified in the area where they offer "free" help. It's not always true, but you usually get what you pay for.

- *Get over the "depersonalization" myth.* The perception that I-Operations will "depersonalize" delivery of products and services subverts the conversion process. Moody Bible Institute in Chicago is pressing ahead with Internet technologies. Joe Stowell, the President, says that every now and then he looks at the letters on file that objected strenuously to their thrust into the new technology of radio, which they have now used successfully for seventy-five years.

The common interface

Internet browsers are becoming the common interface within and between organizations. As more and more companies embrace the reality of operating in the New Economy, intranet and extranet technologies are becoming the common medium of information flows, and Web-enabled, browser accessible applications have quickly become the standard tool.

Statement | **Survey Results**

Internet browsers are becoming the most utilized interface within organizations.

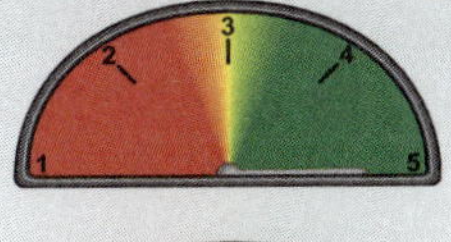

Internet browser applications will be the common link between all parties of interest.

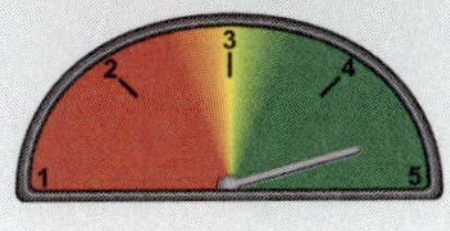

- *Yield individual control to networked leadership.* The CEO of a non-profit must rely upon a well trained and well aligned team instead of his or her passions and rhetoric. This is the most difficult challenge of all. Vision and initiative remain critical, and risks and rewards will vary; but the way forward involves a team that shares authority and responsibility, and embraces investors who expect a certain R.O.I. If your view of leadership is essentially hierarchical, keep looking for a new leadership model.

Myths of Change

- ✓ You can manage change
- ✓ People welcome change
- ✓ Change is simple
- ✓ Change is quick
- ✓ The risks of change can be eliminated
- ✓ We can change on our own
- ✓ Our situation is unique
- ✓ If we have the vision, the details will take care of themselves
- ✓ One day we won't have to change anymore

Source: Christian Management Report[38]

- *Actively pursue outsourcing.* Focus your efforts on the key tasks at hand (the activities to which donors are prepared to contribute money), and outsource the rest to world-class service providers. There are two possible exceptions to this last injunction: first, if you have a "live-learn" philosophy that requires certain non-critical tasks to be performed by staff, and second, if you genuinely cannot afford to outsource.

Academia

The educational arena is confronted with remaining "high-touch" while preparing children and adults for high-tech work. For those universities who are in the heart of the technology belt, such as Stanford University, the challenge is to produce students who have a broad grounding in the liberal arts, and not just the computer sciences. Beyond the two-edged sword of technology, colleges and graduate schools are scrambling to capture the growing continuing education market. Adults 25 and older constitute the vast majority of undergraduate as well as graduate students for distance learning.[39] "Lifetime learning" is no longer a cliché for the liberal arts department, it is an occupational necessity. Administration and faculty trained under 3,000-year-old pedagogical models can find adjustment to the Internet world disconcerting. Yet others are seizing the Internet as a vehicle to extend their reach and slash their costs.

> In 1995, 33 percent of U.S. colleges and universities offered distance courses, according to the Department of Education. In 1998, that figure rose to 44 percent. That translates to about 1.6 million students enrolled in distance-learning programs in the 1997-1998 school year.[40]

Technology may never be a complete substitute for a classroom environment where teacher and students pursue information and insight together. In fact, several schools are and will be marketing themselves as deeply personal, hands-on communities of inquiry. This being said, there is no way to reverse the process of innovation.

Thomas Russell in his aptly named report "No Significant Difference Phenomenon" points out that distance learning yields as many benefits for students as face-to-face instruction.[41]

There are presently four models of academic adaptation. Two of these are extremes that will appeal to fringe markets. The other two are possible ways forward. The first two models are:

- *The "Amish Farm"* academic model. In this setting, computers are a necessary evil and Internet-operations are only used for minimal administrative, marketing and information distribution. This model appeals to a certain "retro-chic" crowd committed to Latin grammar and the Great Books. The danger of this approach is that graduates are ill prepared for a wired world. There are even colleges within an hour of several high-tech centers that remain "unwired". They have a few Web-enabled systems for administration or education, and the distance learning modules still rely on fax machines and snail mail.

- *The "Virtual University"* format. Here all education is through the Web. Sometimes these institutions maintain high standards, and produce excellent leaders and knowledge workers for the Information Age. Graduates of these schools give the institutions high marks for practicality; however, many feel the lack of personal touch and academic depth. The Virtual University is perhaps best illustrated by Cyber State University, a complete Web-based program offering only Information Technology courses. Another example is the University of Phoenix, with cohort-style learning in multiple locations, and Web classes.

It has come under fire for a lack of support resources and teachers that are academically weak. On the other hand, its delivery is attractive to busy professionals.

Somewhere between these two systems lies the ability to integrate the distilled wisdom of world civilizations and the 21st Century skill sets needed for the Internet world. These prior models do not reflect any fundamental internal change. Technological savvy is not a guarantee of innovative leadership structures. The Amish Farm rightly seeks authenticity, but at the cost of relevance.Two other models offer more hope:

- *The Virtual University with the Personal Touch.* The leadership structure is flattened and all faculty and staff have a voice in the direction of the institution. Students have at least sporadic personal contact with leadership and course material is fully Web-based. Personnel and resources are networked around the world. This segment of the academic market will increase as the global village shrinks. Real-time teaching and streaming video is already being piloted. Soon students from all continents will be networked and share a virtual classroom where the teacher and students can all see, hear, and interact with each other.

- *The Community with World Impact.* I-Operations is at the heart of this model because at its core is a commitment to the integration of creative imagination, community impact, career technologies and the call to purposeful and principled living. The centerpiece is a living campus ("bricks") with classrooms wired for learning around the world ("clicks"). Distance learning and cohort programs in other places are the outgrowth of carefully considered plans based

> upon the clear purposes of the institution. Here high-tech and high-touch are not a trade-off. On-campus students utilize the same technology as distance learners around the globe. Administration and faculty create a systemic environment that is dynamic, entrepreneurial and flexible.

This last model is attractive because it retains community and prepares learners for the "Imagination Age" that is built upon emerging technologies and a growing desire to recapture a sense of personal purpose and place (somewhere other than a generic conference room near an airport). The University of Texas is an emerging example of this model.

There are several institutions in the midst of transition from traditional models to one of the four listed above. The birth pangs are sharp, with older leaders resisting the depersonalization of the Internet, and younger leaders failing to capture the camaraderie essential to complete learning.

Towards Integration

The road forward for non-profits entering the 21st Century, including educational institutions, is not too different from that of other businesses. The real challenge is not "tweaking" old paradigms, but creating completely new models that overcome the business/charity dualism and offer a new way of doing good. We are not proposing that charities drop all of their historical assets and try to become businesses. We agree with Peter Drucker, who says that businesses need to become more like charities, and charities more like businesses.

Philanthropic organizations can achieve all of the benefits of I-Operations if they, like their business counterparts, recognize that it is the end-to-end Operating Model that delivers benefit to their target audience.

Looked at another way, non-profit organizations are big on Purpose, but often fail to bring the rest of the Operating Model into alignment with that purpose. Those "administrative" systems, such as donor management, accounting, volunteer scheduling, etc., are every bit as important as handing out food, teaching literacy, digging a well in Africa, or providing an Internet-enabled accounting system for a developing nation charity.

Put New Wine in New Wineskins

A famous historical figure once made an analogy about wine and wineskins saying you should not put new wine in old wineskins because it will damage the old wineskin and waste the new wine.[43] What was he saying? The wineskin is not an end in itself; it is simply the vehicle to get the product to the patrons. One could make the case that the wineskin is the Operating Model. Because there is a regular flow of new wine there is an automatic need for a continuous renewal of the wineskin or Operating Model. There is a triple challenge for non-profits in the faith-based sector today:

- Organizations are vulnerable when they are changing wineskins. Many established non-profits are facing the challenge of passing the baton from the founder to the second (and in many cases third) generation of leaders. (We say third generation because many founders have outlasted the second generation, staying longer than the second generation could bring themselves to stay with the organization, so it is third generation leaders that are taking on the mantle.) The passing of the baton will, in those organizations that are going to survive, result in some changes in the Operating Model.

- The second threat is that this transition is taking place at the same time as the Internet and related shifts are mandating a change in the Operating Model, regardless of whether there is a leadership change.
- The third threat is that founding leaders have been successful precisely because they have prevented their organizations from drifting. While corporate executives go to bed worrying that someone better than them will surpass them, non-profit executives go to bed worrying that their organizations will stray from the path that they as founders have passionately protected. This phenomenon can lead to an increased resistance to change at precisely the time when leadership in a healthy process of change is needed.

If you lead a cause-driven organization and still do not believe that leading into change is difficult, note the words of Jesus of Nazareth, "No one after drinking old wine wants new wine, because he says, `The old wine is better'."[44]

"No one..."—that's not a very comforting statement if the change that you are leading involves a transformation of the Operating Model. So what is the leader of a mission-focused organization to do? And how do you bring about needed change while still maintaining the mission of the organization? Much has been said about the importance of defining corporate values and how these are a guiding light for behavior and corporate ethos. This is true, but founders will come to realize that as clear as these values might be, they are not enough to ensure perpetuity of purpose. Our own story is a case in point.

Prior to the establishing of The Institute we identified our values for the company. We also made some progress in dialoguing the practical implications of such values on how we work and relate. But the day came when we realized that we could have a clear vision and have written values, and the organization could still lose its way. Beyond the good practices of goals, objectives, plans and scorecards, we determined that we needed to document the Foundational Principles upon which The Institute was built. Once this was done, then discussions that brought about necessary changes in the Operating Model could happen without resistance to change lying below the surface out of fear that such change might pull the organization off course. By contrast, we have met leaders of large non-profits who live in fear that the work they started will end in organizational drift and departure from the core mission. History reinforces their fears. Consequently, delegation of authority is difficult, and they have to either micromanage or set up informal decision-making parameters where everyone knows that they make the decision, regardless of what the constitution or organization chart says. The net result is that founder-led and faith-based organizations are often more resistant to change than businesses.

> **"We are not called to be custodians of dusty old bottles or curators of the wineskin museums. We are called to practice flexible supply chain management practices as a necessary condition to continuously getting new wine to new patrons, in a hurry."**
>
> Brett Johnson
> "Structure without Stricture"

Is there an alternative? Instill in your organization the principle that there will always be a segment of the Operating Model under construction. Like the Golden Gate Bridge, assume that some aspect of your organization will always be under scheduled maintenance. And instead of reacting to popped rivets, stretched cables and rust spots in your organization, plan ahead for which areas will be I-Operationalized so that the entire Operating Model—all 10-Ps—is renewed over time.

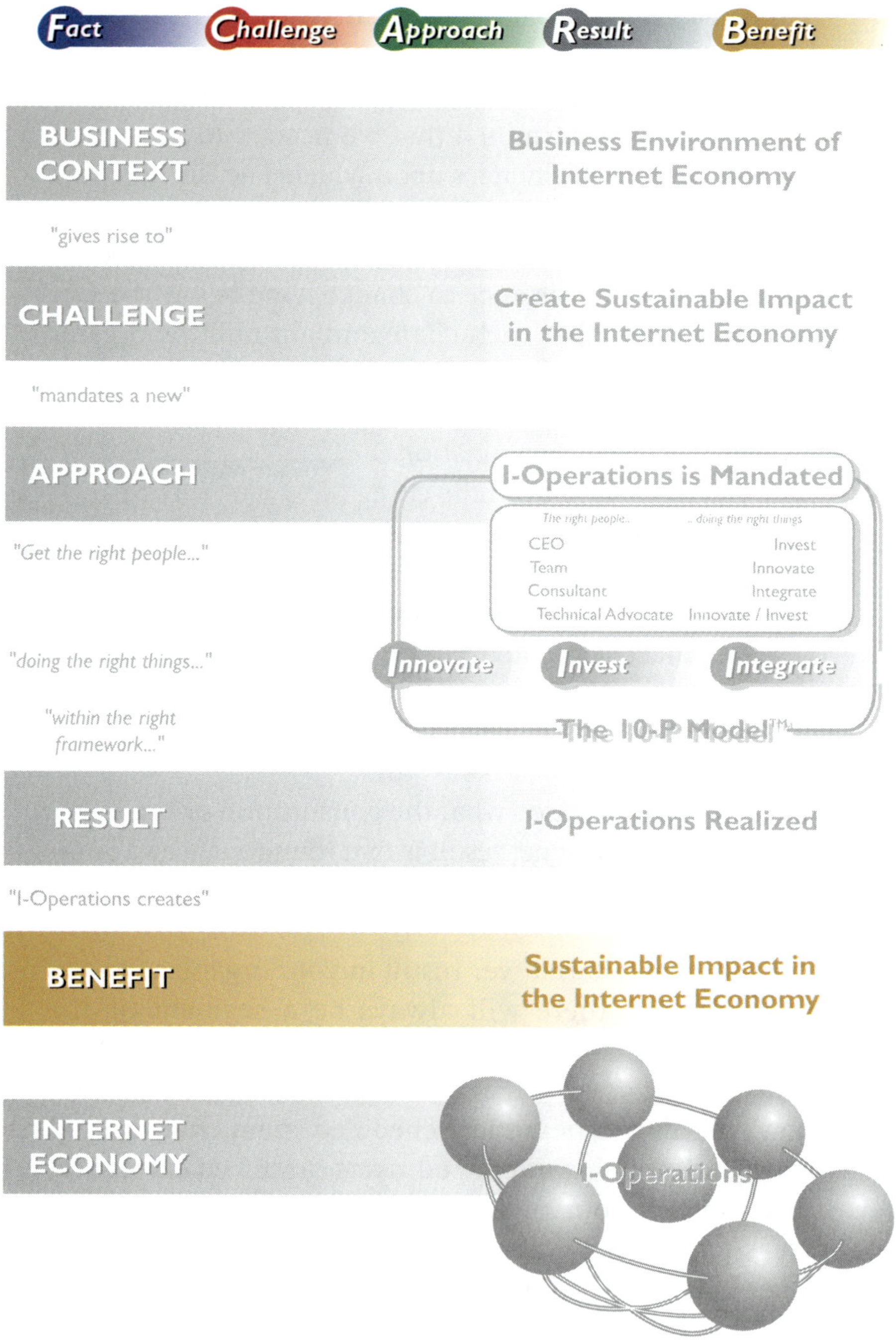
Fact
Challenge
Approach
Result
Benefit
BUSINESS CONTEXT
Business Environment of Internet Economy
"gives rise to"
CHALLENGE
Create Sustainable Impact in the Internet Economy
"mandates a new"
APPROACH
I-Operations is Mandated
The right people...
...doing the right things
CEO
Invest
Team
Innovate
Consultant
Integrate
Technical Advocate
Innovate / Invest
"Get the right people..."
"doing the right things..."
"within the right framework..."
Innovate
Invest
Integrate
The IO-P Model™
RESULT
I-Operations Realized
"I-Operations creates"
BENEFIT
Sustainable Impact in the Internet Economy
INTERNET ECONOMY
I-Operations

Chapter 9

Benefit

Sustainable Impact in the Internet Economy

I-Operations is not an option—it is an imperative. The benefits of I-Operations will vary from one organization to the next, and only you will best understand the specific value of pursuing I-Operations in your own business. Without being experts in all spheres, we would still like to make some suggestions about the potential benefits of embracing I-Operations.

Macro benefits of I-Operations

A recent study by the World Economic Forum (WEF) found that the United States was at the top of the list in terms of global competitiveness. For years Singapore held the top spot, but was edged out by the United States. The main factors used to calculate the ranking are the rate of technological change and rate of capital deepening. Both of these variables are highly multidimensional, and the elements used to determine these growth rates are notable for the sake of this book.

The level of capital includes not just the accumulated physical capital in machinery, structures and physical infrastructure, but also the level of education, workforce skills and attitudes, and managerial talent. The level of technology encompasses not only the technological knowledge embedded in a nation's scientific and technical institutions, but also the technology rooted in organizations. Technology is embodied in every activity an organization performs, as well as in the strategies organizations use to compete.

This is I-Operations on a macro level. While Internet-based technology is essentially leading the revolution in increased productivity, it is not just the adoption of the technology that results in increased productivity. The WEF study shows that skills, education, culture, and management skills are variables that contribute when measuring the level of technology in an economy. Likewise in organizations, technology is merely an enabler of an Operating Model which is supported by good management and a viable value proposition.

Growth Competitiveness Ranking

Country	2002	2001	2000	1999
United States	1	2	1	2
Finland	2	1	6	11
Taiwan	3	7	11	4
Singapore	4	4	2	1
Sweden	5	9	13	19
Switzerland	6	15	10	6
Australia	7	5	12	12

Source: *The Global Competitiveness Report*[45]

The explosion of the Internet in the past decade and the tremendous innovation that has occurred as a result is clearly the driving force of the Internet Economy.

In a world where individuals, communities, and nations were mostly isolated, global GDP grew hardly at all. The invention of the telegraph and railroad in the 19th Century, and then the car, airplane and telephone in the 20th Century allowed ideas to circulate, combine, and recombine in ways never before possible. The result was unprecedented growth in knowledge and wealth. But all of this pales compared to what lies ahead.

> The Internet promises to create a dervishlike dance of intellect, imagination, and capital that is entirely free from the geographical and technological constraints of centuries past. The pace of economic evolution is about to go into hyperdrive.[46]

Organizations are connected like never before. Information flow between companies ignores borders and geography. It is this increase in information sharing that has allowed innovation, and resulted in significant payback.

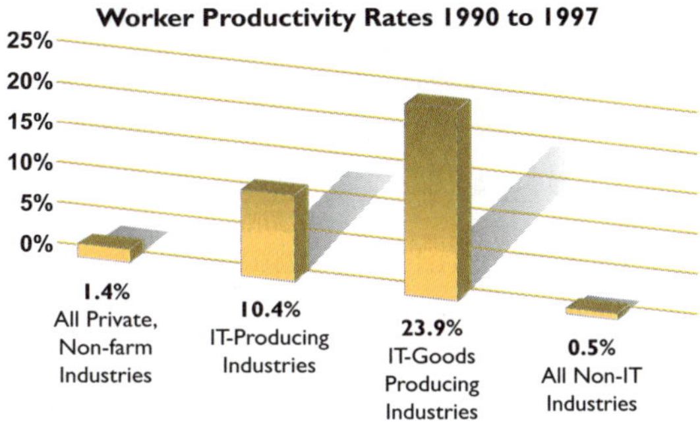

Source: U.S. Department of Commerce.[47]

Still at the macro level, the government of Japan launched its e-Japan initiative in 2001 with nearly $ 17 billion in annual funding plus tax incentives for corporations to build high-speed optical, cable and mobile Internet networks. The less-than-open Japanese market is seeking to attract some 30,000 Internet experts to help create applications that will Internet-enable tax payments, expand e-commerce and service the educational marketplace.

At the micro level, each day there is new proof that organizations with I-Operations are reaping benefits. The productivity of knowledge workers far outstrips that of those involved in non-IT industries. But even this distinction will become less relevant due to the pervasive nature of Internet technologies, and of technology in general.

There is also a strong correlation between creativity, technology and start-ups. Paul David, Economics Professor at Stanford University and Senior Fellow at the Stanford Institute for Economic Policy, states:

> I am convinced that those economists who doubt that there will be significant long-term productivity payoffs from the information revolution will be proved wrong. But those payoffs will not come freely; they will entail much learning and costly organizational changes.[48]

Business benefits of I-Operations

Our research examined the benefits of developing an end-to-end Internet-enabled Operating Model within the business world. Respondents indicated general improvements across a number of fronts. In a Dell Computer press release, Michael Dell states:

> Internet integration to meet operational objectives does lead to improved financial performance. The larger a company is, the more it has to gain by integrating the Internet into its objectives.[49]

The first segment we would like to cover are the so-called "soft areas" that are, in practice, often the difficult areas. As Joseph Stiglitz says, "The process of rethinking how business is conducted itself has a productivity-enhancing effect."[50]

A second set of benefits is related to the core processes of the business, where corporations claimed that they had achieved significant competitive advantage through the deployment of New World Applications. As Eric Lundquist of *eWeek* says, "If your Web efforts aren't geared to making cumbersome processes easier, you are going to find yourself in the Dot-com graveyard."[51]

A third area of benefit is in the Marketing and Sales aspects of the business. Having already indicated that the lines between functions are blurring, there are nonetheless claims that the Internet has resulted in the development of

I-Operations and Competitive Advantage

Our working definition of a New World Application is an application that creates significant competitive advantage for an organization in terms of an increase in the bottom line or an increase in market share. The following results are from companies that were considered to be leaders who responded to the I-Operations Baseline Survey conducted in 2000.

Statement | **Survey Results**

Have any of your network or Internet-based applications created any significant business or competitive advantage for your company?

What types of business or competitive advantages have your network or Internet-based applications created for your company?

- Productivity Gain

- New market entrance

- Market share gain

- Expense/cost reduction

How strongly do you agree that your competition would view your company's Internet-based application as a challenge to their ability to compete with you in this industry?

Stakeholder interaction

The increase in ability to communicate with stakeholders is a clear benefit of Internet applications. Our research indicates that I-Operations companies have the ability to more efficiently interact with external stakeholders. It is likely that as technology develops, there will be newer and better applications deployed to further integrate information flows between companies within an ecosystem.

Statement | **Survey Results**

Internet-enabled applications have enabled us to more efficiently interact with:

- Customers

- Suppliers

- Distributors

- Partners

- Investors

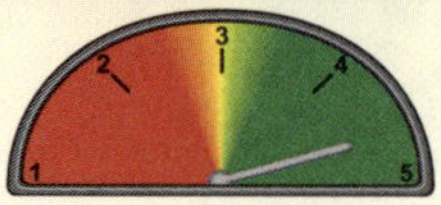

new revenue sources or the enhancement of existing revenue streams. For example:

- The online (computer) gaming industry would not exist without the Internet. While revenues are a fraction of the total industry, they are growing quite quickly.
- Cisco's largest transactions are coming from the Web, topping $32 million in sales everyday.[52]
- Dell generates $50 million in sales each day from it's website.[53]

- Office Depot's worldwide e-commerce sales were over $1.6 billion—14% of sales—and the site has been profitable since its first year of operation.[54]
- Global e-commerce spending has skyrocketed from $50 billion in 1998 to $600 billion in 2001. Projections for 2003 are over $1.3 trillion.[55]

There are also tremendous benefits in the area that has traditionally been called "partnering." We want to be careful when we speak to the benefits of partnering, because it is fraught with misunderstanding. To get a better perspective, we need to look back at the developments in partnering over the past decade or so.

Efficiency gains and Partnering

As the number of I-Operations companies increases, the level of connectivity among partners will increase. Furthermore, as the build out of B2B marketplaces takes place and the move towards Internet-based EDI increases, there will be a significant reduction in transaction costs between companies. Using Internet/network technologies to provide partners with information is viewed by many of our respondents as a significant improvement over traditional means of managing partner relationships.

Statement	Survey Results
Internet /network-based technologies enable us to remove process inefficiencies at the borders between corporations.	
We leverage Internet technologies to manage partners.	

Ten years ago most of the partnering relationships took a long time to develop, were structured around concrete processes and deliverables, were governed by service level agreements, and lasted for a long time. Five years ago there was lots of talk about partnering, with the theories about the end of competition and the development of "ecosystems," and the move from competition to "Co-opetition." But there was a limiting factor that hindered the achievement of that partnering vision, namely, the lack of readily available technologies. Sure there was EDI, but lack of EDI standards made it difficult to deploy. Those brave organizations that pressed ahead with partnering did not experience the success that they hoped for. In fact, five years ago, our estimate is that the Pareto Principle was actually a 90-10 rule when it came to partnering.

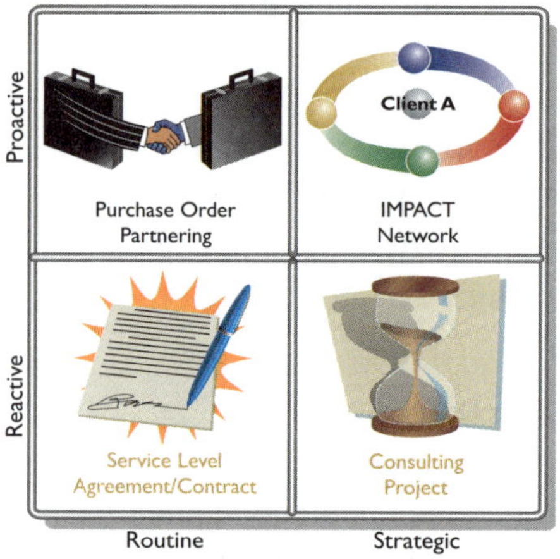

The Internet has become more pervasive, and the notion of partnering has moved from the theoretical to the everyday. There are several reasons for this:

- Internet-related technologies make it much easier to blur the lines between products from different companies. We talked with a software developer who remotely integrated his core product with the software of another Internet company in less than two hours.
- Processes from numerous organizations can be more easily blended. While in-transit assembly of products has been in place in the manufacturing world, we have only begun to scratch the surface of knowledge worker collaborations, even though this is technically easier.
- The communications and cultural barriers between corporations are greatly reduced. For example, a major U.S. corporation has multi-organizational project teams that have websites for specific sales initiatives. Beyond this, they are open to international team members on the public Internet, without password protection. Their rationale: no

one who is not part of the team will ever find them. The reticence to sharing information across organizations and countries is greatly reduced.

In 1997, The Institute developed a term to describe this new type of partnering; we called it an Impact Network™. This is the subset of organizations that you pull from the universe of players to repeatedly help you create an impact. The rationale then was that it takes a network to achieve impact. This is even truer today. Clients or customers no longer believe that one company has it all. Customers therefore expect that their suppliers will work together to develop the solutions that they need.

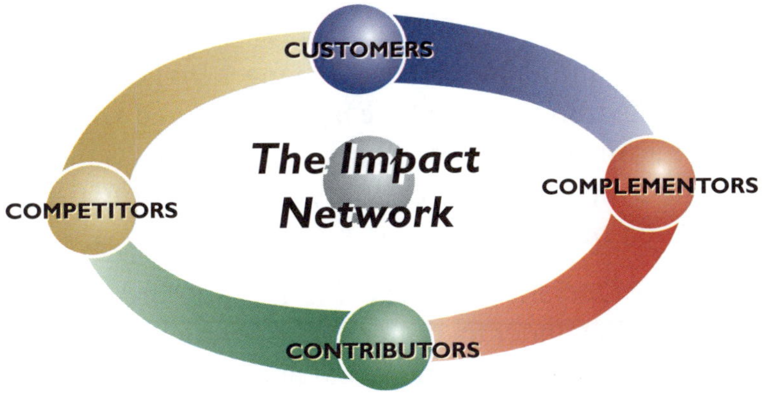

The Impact Network has four cardinal points: Customers, Competitors, Contributors (or suppliers), and Complementors.

While larger corporations sometimes have the luxury of acquiring smaller companies that fill gaps in their product architecture, this does not eliminate the need for partnering. The beauty of the Internet is that it makes it possible for organizations to deliberately design and build cross-corporation networks that generate enhanced value for customers. The cross-selling between companies in the travel industry where airlines offer car rentals, and car rental companies offer hotel rooms is an example of Internet-enabled collaboration across the Impact Network.

Benefits of I-Operations in the Social Sector

Today many social sector organizations are overcoming past inefficiencies and are developing I-Operations. E-government is becoming more prevalent, and Asian countries are sending representatives to Western cities to study this phenomenon. Five things are happening at once in the social sector:

- There have been dramatic improvements in relational networking among organizations that share a common passion thanks largely to the improved communications brought about by the Internet.

- The equivalent of B2B Exchanges for the philanthropic world are being pioneered where information is freely shared, and donors wanting to support field projects are able to identify field projects that meet their giving criteria.

- The Operating Models of non-profits are slowly coming under the influence of Internet-related technologies. Practices that are everyday in business are beginning to be more commonplace in social sector organizations. Customer relationship management is becoming more sophisticated, and a new wave of ASPs that outsource the back end "business functions" of non-profits is about to sweep over the non-profit world.

- The motivational or cause related aspects of non-profits are emerging in for-profit corporations. For example, cause related marketing in businesses has increased significantly in recent years, and will continue to do so. This is highlighting the benefit of collaboration between business and social sectors, and knowledge transfer is a natural consequence.

- The lines between for-profit and non-profit organizations are blurring. A new wave of mega donors is beginning to question the necessity and efficiency of being a "registered charity" in order to get charitable work done. Many are questioning whether it even makes sense. The possibilities of "doing well while doing good" are increasing each day. And where separate charitable organizations still make sense, corporations are setting up charities that can express the company's desire to make a difference.

Another benefit in the social sector is that the Internet is facilitating collaboration between corporations and charities. The level of volunteerism is rising in the U.S. Workers are more informed about social needs in their communities, and some of the service opportunities, such as tutoring, can be achieved over the Internet. Many companies have begun training programs in schools to train high school students in technical skills. The Cisco Networking Academies operate in thousands of schools around the world, many located in least developed countries, providing students who complete the 285 hours of training with practical networking skills. The students, the schools and the business world benefit from this type of partnership.[56]

The principle of having a corporate purpose that includes yet extends beyond profit making is beginning to take root in businesses. Government entities are seeing the value of being customer focused. Faith based organizations are seizing the opportunity to toss out tired traditions and renew their wineskins. And individuals are seeking a cohesion between work life and the rest of living.

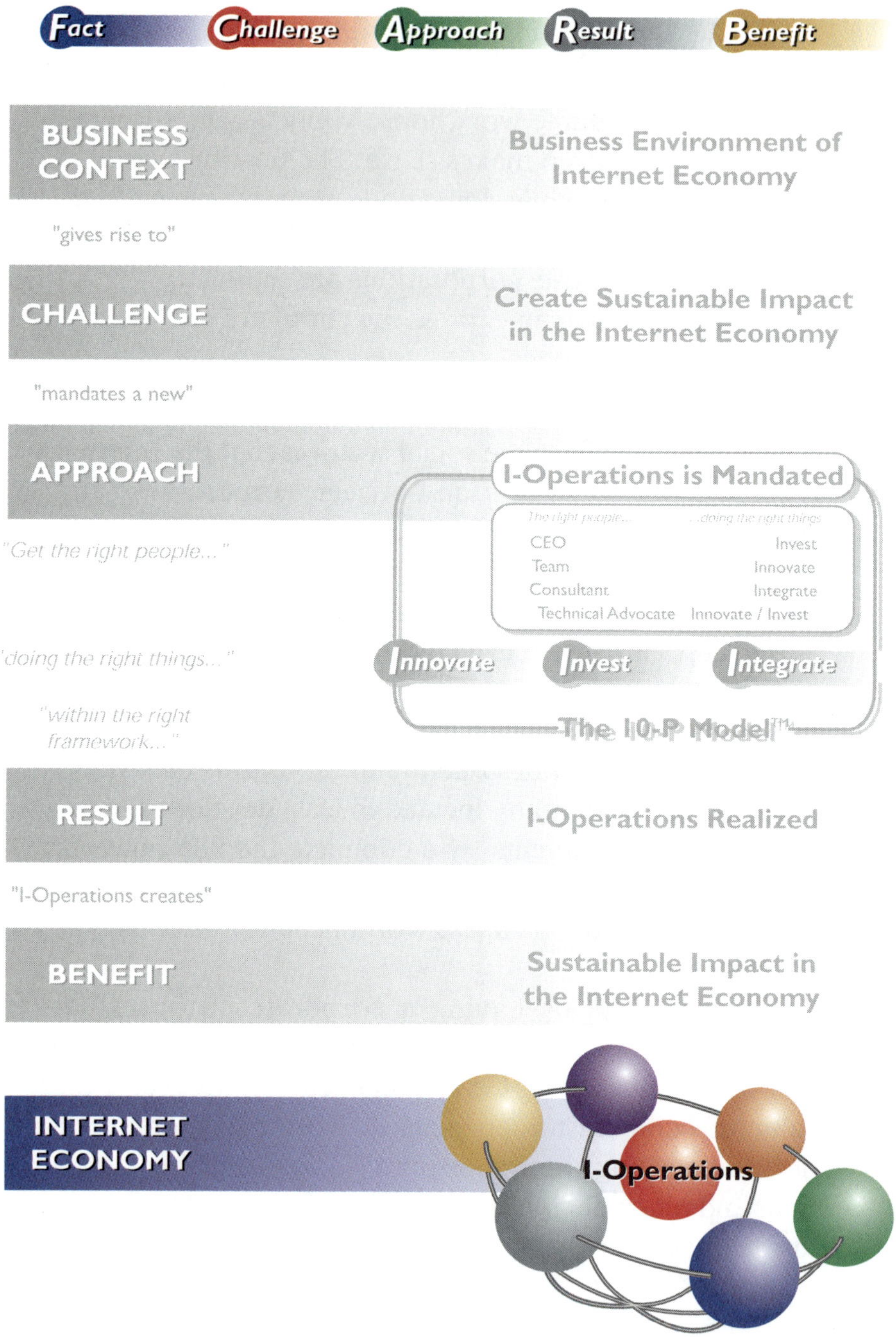

Fact
Challenge
Approach
Result
Benefit
BUSINESS CONTEXT
Business Environment of Internet Economy
"gives rise to"
CHALLENGE
Create Sustainable Impact in the Internet Economy
"mandates a new"
APPROACH
I-Operations is Mandated
"Get the right people..."
The right people...
...doing the right things
CEO
Invest
Team
Innovate
Consultant
Integrate
Technical Advocate
Innovate / Invest
"doing the right things..."
Innovate
Invest
Integrate
"within the right framework..."
The I0-P Model™
RESULT
I-Operations Realized
"I-Operations creates"
BENEFIT
Sustainable Impact in the Internet Economy
INTERNET ECONOMY
I-Operations

Chapter 10

I-Operations

A Personal Look at I-Operations

This chapter diverges from the statistical research to explore the personal implications of the Internet for leaders. It is obviously based upon our perspective of leadership and how the Internet is making a leader's value system more visible to the world. It alerts readers to the fact that the Internet seldom confines itself to the neat categories of "business" and "personal" life. We therefore propose a framework for dialogue about integrated thinking on this subject.

Internet technologies are at once personal and pervasive. Previous waves of technology were not as boundless as the Internet. Few people took their Enterprise Resource Planning system home with them. Few used the corporation's data warehouse from their laptop machine at home. While a limited number used systems such as Sales Force Automation, the technology was tailored to a particular company and was nowhere near as ubiquitous as Internet technologies. Why is this personal nature of the Internet important? Because the same technologies are being used to surf the Internet at home and manage corporate data at work, to access e-mail at home and work, to perform research about an upcoming vacation and research about a vendor of widgets... the Internet eliminates many of the technological barriers between home and work, and vice versa. Mobile technologies that leverage the Internet are especially pervasive. And the elimination of barriers does not stop at technology. Cultural barriers are likewise being dismantled. The boundaries of communication style, dress code, working hours vs. leisure hours and attitudes towards hierarchy, to name a few, are becoming less relevant.

With this comes a tremendous opportunity to take the positive aspects of home and leisure, and bring them into work life. Likewise, a raft of management tools previously within the domain of work are now available for homes: Internet-based asset management, financial management, communications, time management, etc.

The potential effects of the Internet go beyond the tools and technologies. Because the definition of work-life is up for grabs, Internet-related trends cause us to re-examine how life hangs together. In an interview with FAST COMPANY, Peter Koestenbaum, a classically trained philosopher with degrees in philosophy, physics, and theology from Stanford, Harvard and Boston University, articulates some of these challenges.

> We're living in a peculiar time: It's marked by ... the creation of tremendous wealth, an explosion in innovation, and the acute alienation that occurs when the global economy hits the average individual. What I call the "new economy-pathology" is driven by impossible demands—better quality, lower prices, faster innovation—that generate an unprecedented form of stress. People feel pressure to meet ever-higher objectives in all realms of work, wealth, and lifestyle—and thrive on that pressure in the process.[57]

This meshing of work and home, Career and Community, has implications for leaders of corporations. First, it implies that the skills of leaders need to be sharpened to handle people management in a way that was not anticipated in the past. And "management" may be too strong a word because many Net-savvy workers resist overly directive management styles.

Second, it means that employees are juggling a complex set of variables in their continual internal dialogue about whether to join or stay at a company. The fluid job market coupled with internal uncertainties causes many knowledge workers to join a company, browse for a while, and then leave after a month or two.

> Change—true, lasting, deep-seated change—is the business world's biggest and most persistent challenge. But too many people and too many companies approach change by treating it as a technical challenge rather than developing authentic answers to basic questions about business life.[58]

A third implication of the blurring of boundaries between work and other spheres of life is that workers are increasingly attuned to and critical of inconsistencies in the corporate and private lives of their leaders.

Until now, we have discussed the Ten Drivers of Impact as spokes in a wheel. The limitation of this analogy is that it leaves corporations with unicycles rather than racing bikes. And given the personal nature of Internet technologies and the implications for corporations, we need a second wheel on our bicycle.

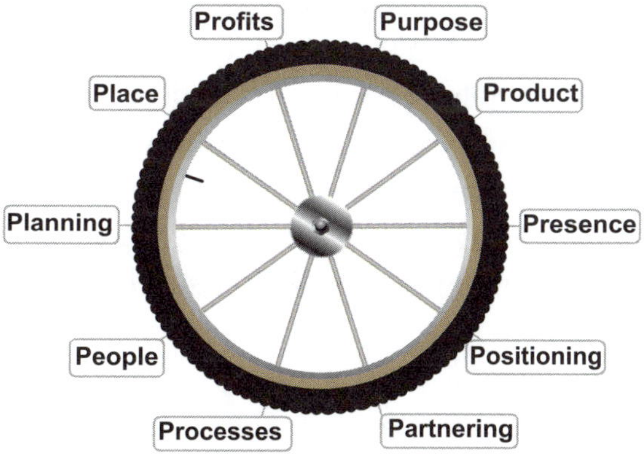

Second wheel of the leader

The blending of corporate and private worlds means that we have to pay attention to the personal wheel as much as the corporate wheel. We have seen the catastrophic results of leaders who have tremendous corporate skills, but lack character. Likewise, there have been many leaders who have excellent character credentials, but lack the basic skills that are needed to lead and manage a corporation. Peter Koestenbaum has this to say about the duality of leadership:

> Think of leadership as the sum of two vectors: competence (your specialty, your skills, your know-how) and authenticity (your identity, your character, your attitude). When companies and people get stuck, they tend to apply more steam—more competence—to what got them into trouble in the first place... The problem is, when you're stuck, you're not likely to make progress by using competence as your tool. Instead, progress requires commitment to two things. First, you need to dedicate yourself to understanding yourself better... Second, you need to change your habits of thought...[59]

The 10-P Model that we introduced earlier provides a framework for fresh thinking about critical components of a corporation. It helps provide a loom on which we can weave our "habits of thought." To follow Koestenbaum's admonition to "understand yourself better" and "change your habits of thought," we need a framework that will encompass the personal as well as the corporate.

Before expanding on this model, let us share its origins. In the early 1990s, while holding regular meetings with a group of entrepreneurs, we began to discuss the issues of balancing work and home life. At the core of this challenge was the fact that people were running low on what Dr. Richard Swensen calls "Margin." A medical doctor, Swensen observed that a majority of his patients had conditions that were the direct result of running out of rope, be it financial, emotional, physical or spiritual rope. Over a period of years, we incorporated the idea of margin into a model that we had been developing, called The 10-F Model™. This model has been verified with numerous groups and individuals of all ages ranging from CEOs to people in Third World communities. There are ten spokes in the personal wheel that are critical to sustainable impact in individuals. The areas in the personal wheel can be examined in several different ways:

- *Margin*—We need to have margin in each of the ten areas in order to have impact. If we are continuously out of slack in any of these areas, our ability to be effective will be hampered.

- *Contentment*—The question is not so much how much we have, but how content we are with what we have. On finances, for example, we can have more than enough, but if we are not content with what we have, we will be driven to make choices or pursue activities that erode well-rounded life effectiveness.

- *Completeness*—Do we have all of the spokes in the wheel? Do they reach the rim? Do we have the personal characteristics needed to ensure that the corporate strategies we have set in place are not undermined by personal gaps?

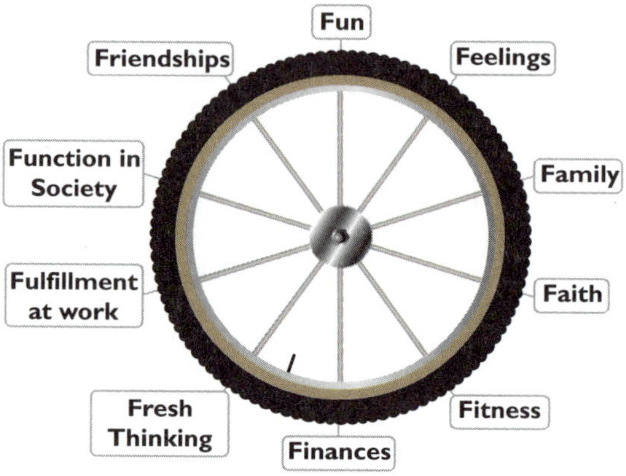

In his article entitled "The Psychological Underpinnings of the 10-Fs," psychologist Dr. Art Wouters, has this to say:

> The 10-Fs represent a system of thinking about the lives of individuals. The 10-Fs comprise a model that is both theoretical and practically applicable. The model was developed by The Institute as a way of giving persons access to the defining areas of their lives. It is frequently used as an assessment tool to enable business and organizational leaders to reflect on the impact, contentment, and the degree of margin in the personal dimensions of their lives.[60]

The 10–Fs are fairly self-explanatory:

Fun	...remember the blurring of the distinction between leisure and work.

Fulfillment at work	...people are increasingly thinking about meaning at work.
Function in Society	...and what my role will be in my community, local and global.
Fresh Thinking	... people are born to create, and they are personally rejuvenated when they are in environments of fresh thinking.
Finances	... not *Who wants to be a Millionaire?*, but the ability to earn and manage adequate finances.
Fitness	... a lack of fitness drains the juice out of other areas of life.
Friendships	... we look for and need connections with others.
Feelings	... how we feel about ourselves. A short spoke leaves us susceptible to less-than-optimal living.
Faith	a belief system... "religious faith remains one of the most understudied social phenomena of the 20th Century," according to Princeton University President, Harold Shapiro.[61]
Family	... the single biggest factor in turning out mentally healthy kids—eating dinner with their families at least 5 times a week.[62]

One-wheel leaders

The 2000 Presidential election in the U.S. was a striking example of the dilemma of having to choose between front wheel and back wheel leaders. George W. Bush was portrayed as a man who had a "good heart." The implication was that Bush did not have relevant experience. Al Gore was portrayed as someone who had good head knowledge, but did not have the character to go with it. Setting aside their philosophical differences, the close election perhaps reflects America's desire for a leader that has both wheels.

History is littered with leaders who were creative, even had a certain genius, but lacked the front wheel of the leader. Their charisma was not matched with character. Even in our "modern" world where people have become far more tolerant of a broad diversity of opinions on morality and ethics, the majority of people feel slighted when the personal integrity and conduct of a leader does not match up to the requirements of their office, be that in business, government, or the non-profit sector. But what does the Internet have to do with leadership?

Transparency of leadership

> To be persuasive we must be believable; to be believable we must be credible; to be credible we must be truthful.
>
> —Edward R. Murrow

The Internet brings a heightened sense of immediacy to the dynamics of leadership. Stock prices soar on the basis of a smart acquisition, and they slump when a company fails to meet analyst expectations for quarterly earnings. CEOs can be heroes one day, and villains the next.

Further, the mistakes and the successes of leaders are more readily apparent in the Internet Era. There is little assurance that deep dark secrets will remain hidden in an age where e-mails—true or not—travel unhindered from cube to customer to competitor at the speed… well, almost of light. A *Wall Street Journal* article in March 2000 told the story of a CEO who sent a terse e-mail to managers about employee work hours. "Hell will freeze over before this CEO implements another employee benefit in this Culture... You have a problem and you will fix it or I will replace you..." The point here is not the statement itself (which is not the norm in the U.S. business culture), but the fact that in this Internet Era such statements are apparent to anyone with an Internet browser. A short while after the internal e-mail was sent, it appeared on a Yahoo! website, was the subject of chat room chatter, and the company's stock dropped 28%. To make matters worse, the company had already been chosen by *Fortune* magazine as one of the "100 best companies to work for in America."

We have already made the case that internal and external stakeholders have an improved view into the organization. With this, corporations are effectively providing such stakeholders with the tools to hold the corporation's feet to the fire. When you let suppliers monitor your inventory levels in order to supply you better, then you open the quality of your inventory management practices to their scrutiny.

You might argue, "Surely if I get the job done, my character should not be at issue." That's just the point. In a wired, immediate-information world—remembering that the lines between work and life as a whole are blurring—you won't be able to get the job done without two wheels on your bicycle.

Framework for integrated leadership

We now have two wheels, the Corporate and the Personal. The question then remains, how do we keep these two wheels aligned? Bicycles don't mysteriously hang together; there are components besides the wheels.

The frame of Integration holds the two wheels of leaders together. Beyond just holding them together, the frame has to ensure that the wheels remain aligned—they both have to be consistent with, and directly contributing to, the desired impact of the organization. A lot of attention has been given to enhancing the benefits packages—with the possible exception of vacation time or "Personal Days"—of high-tech workers in the U.S. in recent years. In-house chefs, dry cleaners, and more are all an attempt to make life at work more…well, more! Keeping employees over the long haul requires more than soft-side perks; it requires leaders with an integrated view of personal and business life.

The cyclist still must decide where the bike should go. The leader likewise will have to make informed choices about where the organization is headed. For purposes of this illustration, we will avoid the debate about how many people have their hands on the handlebars. We have already explained that achieving I-Operations happens when a cast of characters plays different and complementary roles. Our point here is that a leading corporation must have a clear idea of the impact that they want to have. A specific definition of desired future impact determines direction.

Continuing the bicycle analogy, a cyclist entering the Olympic Games today with a bicycle from 1950 has no chance of competing successfully with the old bulbous tires, the heavy materials, the wall-to-wall mudguards, etc. Perhaps the biggest drawback, however, would be the absence of a sophisticated set of gears. In our analogy, this is the Innovation. Gearing enables a long-distance cyclist to adapt to changing terrain, wind conditions, and competitive challenges almost instantaneously. Multi-faceted innovation ensures that a leader stays abreast of, if not ahead of, the times. In our model, innovation must be a constant across all 10-Ps and all 10-Fs if we are to be effective. This—together with an integrated framework and the right investments—is what allows organizations and individuals to achieve impact.

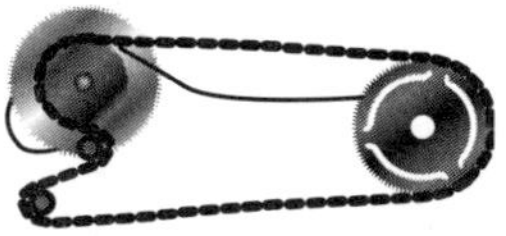

Investment is the final component of our bicycle. Investment is the fourth I of the bicycle, and it is the pedals. The pedals are where you move from theory to practice. It's what takes you from being a roof rack cyclist to a cyclist. Participation in the 21st Century requires an investment at the personal level as well as at the corporate level. Beyond the buzzwords of lifelong learning and continuous retraining, leaders must have a solid grasp of the implications of people as assets. (The suggestion of valuing pre-IPO companies on the basis of dollars million per employee is a practical indicator that people are the real assets of corporations.) In Chapter 6 we covered the basics of the investment required to implement I-Operations. This investment was essentially focused on the second or rear wheel of the corporation.

What types of investments should you make in the front wheel to remain an impact player? Before we pose some questions you might ask yourself, it is important to spell out a few principles:

- Investing in people is not about quick techniques to squeeze a better return out of employees.
- One of the principal jobs of a leader is that of Corporate Storyteller. Perhaps the title of CEO should be changed to CSO—Chief Storytelling Officer.

- Leaders must be consistent with their stories. You must be believed to be heard. The title CSO could be a two-edged sword if the front wheel of the leader is out of alignment with his or her back wheel.
- Some of the investments in the front wheel are soft investments. But the soft investments are often the most difficult investments for leaders to make. Some examples are: speaking words of encouragement, noticing extra effort, conveying thanks. "The first responsibility of a leader is to define reality. The last is to say thank you. In between the leader must become a servant and a debtor. That sums up the progress of an artful leader."[63]
- As you can see, many investments do not cost much money. In their book *Encouraging the Heart*, James Kouzes and Barry Posner list 150 ways to encourage the heart; most of them require more from your own heart than the corporate coffers.

In a changing world, it is good to rethink the questions that could lead to good investments in the front wheel of our organizations.

"F" spoke	Investment questions
Fun	How can fun activities at work be connected to the purpose of the organization?
Fulfillment at work	What is the best way to ensure that people's work is aligned with their natural talents?

Function in Society	How does the Internet create new opportunities for community involvement, perhaps with work as the springboard? How can our corporation take on a deliberate community role that is consistent with our business purpose?[64]
Fresh Thinking	How does the Internet create new opportunities for employees to expand their thinking?
Finances	How has the Internet shaped people's views of Finances? How do we build a long-term corporate plan amidst short term ("Internet years") thinking... one that meets the employee and the corporate needs?
Fitness	Do we frown on people taking time out for fitness, or do we encourage it?
Friendships	How do we recognize new expressions of Internet community, foster community at work, and still encourage staff to nurture relationships outside of the corporation?
Feelings	How do we best encourage the hearts of staff and create a connection between their emotions and the corporate story?
Faith	With numerous trends pointing towards a resurgence of spirituality and the de-emphasizing of the physical constructs of religious institutions, how do we allow for the integration of faith into the life of corporations? How do we explore the connections between faith and risk?

Family	How do we mitigate the negative impacts of the Internet on Family? How do we leverage the Internet to be a unifying factor in families? How do we manage the boundaries around "work as family"?

Earlier we looked at some of the corporate and technology trends being fueled by the Internet. There is a similar set of personal trends that is greatly impacted by technology. At the heart of these trends is the blurring of the lines between areas of life, which we have deemed to be separate since the Industrial Revolution.

Trend[65]	**Implications**
Work as Community: Some corporations are attempting to create a home-like atmosphere for work. People at Mrs. Grossman's Paper Company decorate their factories any way they please. With job security no longer an option, smart employers are turning in other directions to make work seem more like a community.	The softening of the hard edges between home and work will allow the fortunate few to overcome the schism between work and home. This places new pressures on the workplace to be more to people, and could result in a not-so-healthy redefining of what home is. For those corporations who recognize this, allowing potted plants and pets won't be enough to reflect this trend. If the practices of the company are not aligned with the stated core values of the organization, workers will detect this schism more quickly than ever.

Globalization: People from around the world can compete for your job, and most of them for less money. People living outside your native country can research and apply for a job around the corner from you just as easily as you can, thanks to information available on the Internet.	One has to continuously re-tool in order to maintain sought after skills. Competitive advantage in the workplace at the worker level has often come from one individual having information that others did not have. Now one can assume that others have access to as much information as you do. So what makes the difference? As someone commented, "I hire people for skills; I fire them for lack of character."
The shifting location of education: Education originally began in the home. Religious institutions then assumed the education role, with a later shift to public schools.	In recent years, corporations have taken on the role of educator: With the availability of home-accessible information via the Internet, will this fuel the shift of education back to the home? And with the growing information empowerment of The Millennial Generation (Y), will they self-manage more of their education? This emboldened self-management of education may be a pre-cursor to the self-management of Careers.

What we might do tomorrow doesn't exist today: Many of the 21st Century jobs don't exist today. Rapid changes in technology will make obsolete much of what we considered to be "bedrock of society" jobs.

We need to pay closer attention to the creative side of our lives. Our ability to adapt and reinvent ourselves will be key to our success.

The quest for creativity in work, and meaning in play: "In the Dream Society, free time will occasionally be difficult to distinguish from work and—above all—it will be imbued with emotional content..."[66]

On the down side, our children will see us as constantly working. ("That wasn't a vacation... you were working.")
On the plus side, there will be a vastly expanded number of opportunities to find or create jobs that embrace our creativity.

"In the future, the distinction between work and spare time will wither away—because, increasingly, the demands we put on our leisure time will be the same ones we put on our work. We are approaching a fully integrated life."[67]

People will seek jobs with greater meaning, and spend more time working at such jobs. But the distinctions between such work and play will blur. Working holidays will increase, people will find it harder to discern true priorities, and without a stable values base, people will be more sold-out than ever to their Career.

These are just a few examples of trends that underline the importance of having an integrated view of work. Put another way, when the nature of how we work and play becomes indistinguishable, 100% of what we do is work. We simply don't get paid for all of the time we spend working. Many years ago, someone said, "America is where we work at play, worship our work, and play at worship." As we get ankle-deep into the Internet Era, even this segregated criticism of life will be challenged. The ubiquitous nature of the enabling technology will flat-out minimize these hard distinctions we have for separate buckets of life, and we will be forced to find a philosophical framework that allows for integration.

Practical application of the Bicycle model

Many companies have orientation programs for new employees that go beyond the basics of filling in medical forms and finding the restrooms. At The Institute, employee orientation is preceded by a virtual internship. This is an e-mail dialogue with prospective recruits that attempts to ensure that people we interview are aligned with our values and dreams. Once recruits have progressed through this funnel and have been hired, they complete a self-assessment (verified by Human Resources) of their 10-Fs and 10-Ps. This is then used to plan and monitor personal progress. Why is this important? In "The Psychological Underpinnings of the 10-F Model," Dr. Wouters states:

> The process of choosing relies on the assumptions of human responsibility and therefore the significance of exercising one's independent will. We have to choose, even if we are unable to obtain all the facts and guarantee its success. The act of commitment to change is in itself a powerful

> force that propels us toward success. The 10-F system relies heavily on these therapeutic change processes of consciousness raising and choosing. The system assumes that individuals are capable of making meaningful self-assessments that raise awareness and lead to appropriate choices for changing their lives.[68]

Whatever model your corporation may choose to use, it is important to assess the impacts of trends—and especially technology-driven, Internet-related trends—on people as individuals and employees. It is also crucial to recognize that, in part because of the technology-enabled cultural shifts, the separation of people-as-people and people-as-employees is eroding. Thankfully. The picture of the bicycle provides thinking tools to further the process of asking the right questions, even if it is too early to know the right answers. And the rate of technological, cultural and Operating Model change will guarantee that we will need to be asking new questions for some time to come.

Do leaders have to be perfect? We will do better to recognize that they will not be. Is it a must for leaders to have both skills and character? It is for those corporations who want to have sustainable impact. The most successful of ancient Israel's kings did not have a squeaky clean record, but the psalmist has this to say to David's credit:

> And David shepherded them with integrity of heart [the front wheel of the leader]; with skillful hands [the back wheel] he led them.[69]

The personal implications of the Internet cause us to ask questions of ourselves: "Can we implement skills for good without character? What 'assets of character' do we possess that enabled the development of our skills in the first place? How might we more deliberately deploy character for the corporate good? And how might the advent of the Internet promote a leadership 'package' that is a brighter blend of character and competence?"

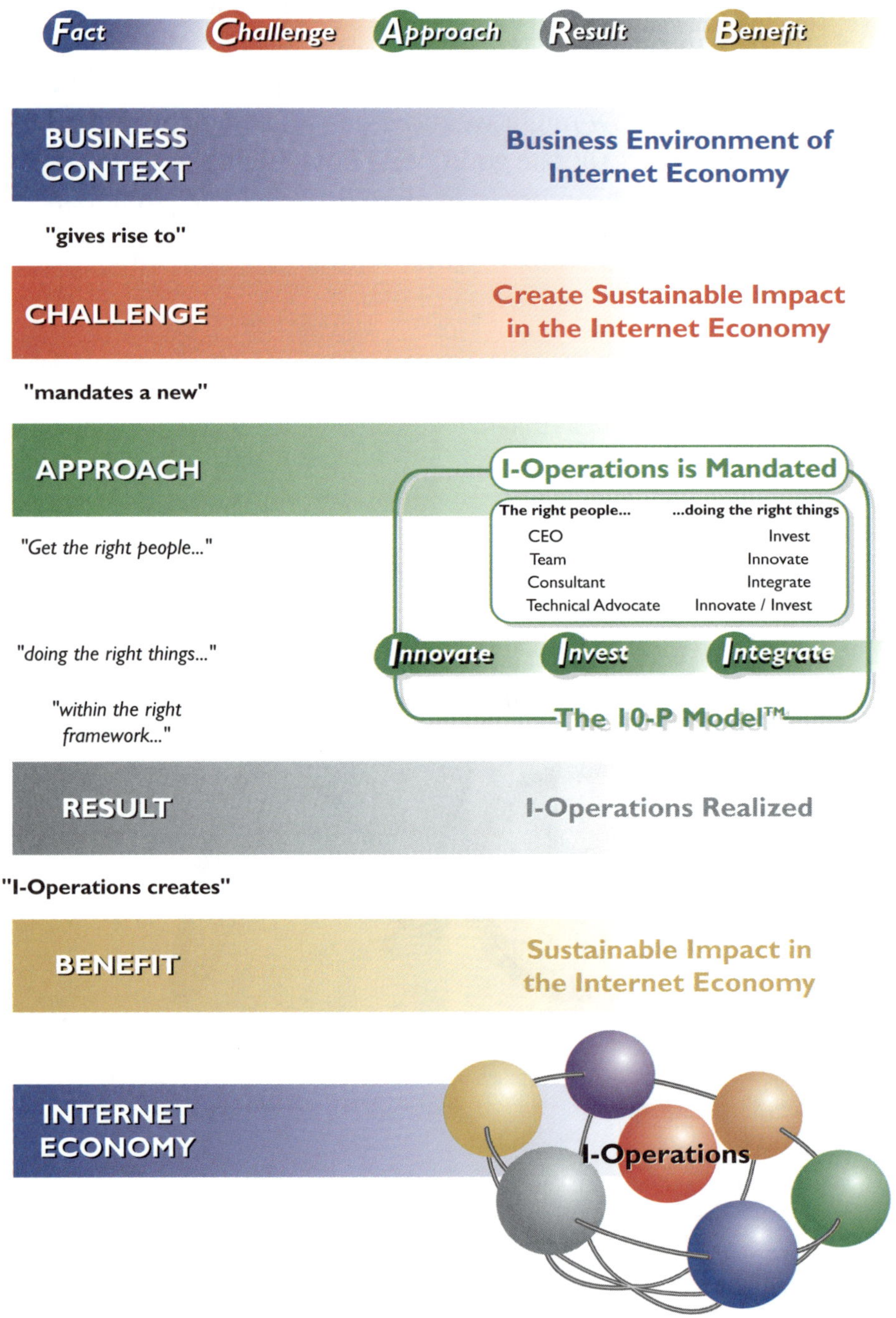

Fact
Challenge
Approach
Result
Benefit
BUSINESS CONTEXT
Business Environment of Internet Economy
"gives rise to"
CHALLENGE
Create Sustainable Impact in the Internet Economy
"mandates a new"
APPROACH
I-Operations is Mandated
The right people...
...doing the right things
CEO
Invest
Team
Innovate
Consultant
Integrate
Technical Advocate
Innovate / Invest
"Get the right people..."
"doing the right things..."
"within the right framework..."
Innovate
Invest
Integrate
The 10-P Model™
RESULT
I-Operations Realized
"I-Operations creates"
BENEFIT
Sustainable Impact in the Internet Economy
INTERNET ECONOMY
I-Operations

Chapter 11

Conclusion

As we conclude this book, we want to mention a few caveats. While we are excited about the possibilities that the Internet brings, we must also be realistic. It is our personal view that the business cycle is not dead. We believe this economy will present great success and also great challenge. It is therefore important that we make several statements, even though they are blindingly obvious to many readers:

- The Internet Economy is not necessarily a good economy for everyone, yet it is the New Economy in which we will all conduct our business.
- The Internet Economy, in our definition, is not necessarily synonymous with a new era of economics where we have unending expansion and good fortune for all.
- The Internet Economy is also not just a bubble economy.

Despite these disclaimers, we believe that I-Operations is important for all corporations in the future, regardless of what happens to economic indicators. Our ability to weather economic storms will be improved if our organizations have the characteristics we have come to associate with I-Operations:

- Cultural agility
- Organizational flexibility
- Process fluidity
- Improved communications
- Quicker decision-making
- Improved response times
- Meaningful and plentiful partnering.

Pulling it all together

I-Operations, like all good business practice, must focus on the customer. Trends in today's world have, however, increased the importance of Internal as well as External stakeholders. Customers are, therefore, at the center of the I-Operations model.

We have already established that the nature of Operating Models has changed from the linear to the circular model. Put another way, all aspects of the Operating Model have become customer-facing, and the distinction between back end and front end applications is being eliminated. This continuous and potentially seamless Operating Model wraps around external and internal customers.

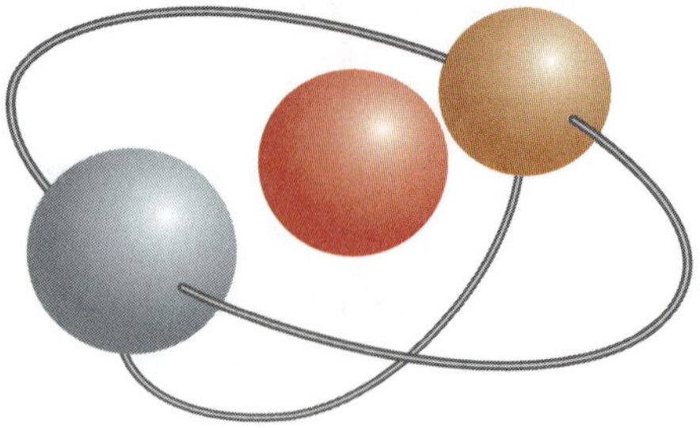

All aspects of the Operating Model are geared towards—or aligned around—the fulfillment of the Purpose of the organization. There is therefore end-to-end alignment in this cohesive Operating Model that encompasses all ten corporate and all ten personal Drivers of Impact.

In theory, one can have a complete Operating Model that serves customers and is not supported by technology at all. The greengrocer's store of 100 years ago is an example. But in the Internet Economy, corporations that will be successful are those whose Operating Models are enabled by Internet-related technologies, precisely because these technologies foster significant advantages over previous methods of conducting business. In I-Operations, the Operating Model is enabled by Internet technologies and utilizes New World Applications.

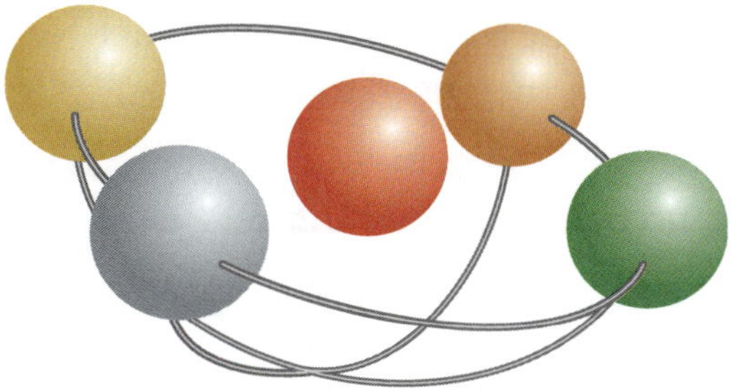

Applications and technologies are very real things. We can see them, touch them, and sense them. Our definition of an Operating Model extends to areas of values, culture and communications. We have concluded that it is helpful to emphasize that the benefits of I-Operations will probably not be realized if the more concrete aspects of the applications and operations are not infused with "softer" elements of Internet Culture.

The fresh thinking needed to envision new ways in which to create a New World customer experience will generally not come without a New World culture. The fact that we are seeing a collision of trends from multiple spheres means that we need to pay particular attention to Internet Culture as we complete the picture on what it takes to have a successful corporation.

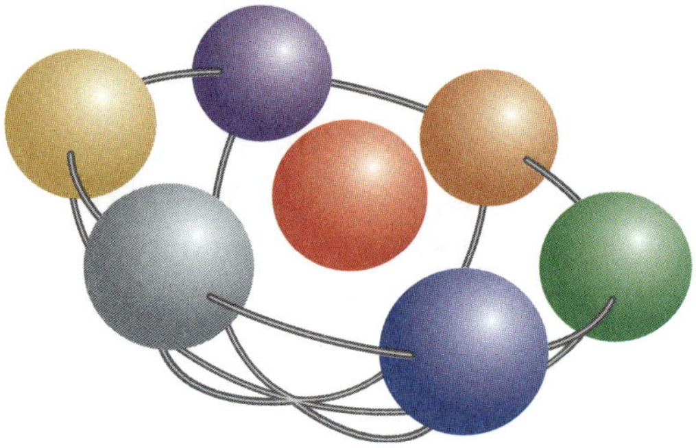

Is there an alternative?

We do not promise that achieving the I-Operations your corporation needs will be cheap, easy, or fast. We do know, as do all serious observers, that we are living in a world where all of the players in our Impact Network are more informed that they used to be:

- *Customers:* The majority of customers first research major purchases on the Internet before visiting a store.
- *Internal Customers:* Employees have a window to executive leaders that was not there before.
- *Competitors:* Your competition can know more about you in five minutes than they could have in five months just a short while ago.
- *Complementors:* As the world of collaboration increases, your supply chain and other partners see the good and bad side of your operations almost immediately. Notice how quickly an inventory shortage of, say, a computer component ripples through the related corporations, and through Wall Street.

These are just a few examples which illustrate the fact that "you can run, but you can't hide." Organizations can tweak the components of the Operating Model, but unless they embrace and implement I-Operations, they will not be successful. And this is equally true for businesses, academic institutions, governments, and the social sector. All modern corporations need I-Operations, now.

Fact **Challenge** **Approach** **Result** **Benefit**

BUSINESS CONTEXT — **Business Environment of Internet Economy**

"gives rise to"

CHALLENGE — **Create Sustainable Impact in the Internet Economy**

"mandates a new"

APPROACH — **I-Operations is Mandated**

"Get the right people..."

The right people...	**...doing the right things**
CEO	Invest
Team	Innovate
Consultant	Integrate
Technical Advocate	Innovate / Invest

"doing the right things..."

Innovate **Invest** **Integrate**

"within the right framework..."

The 10-P Model™

RESULT — **I-Operations Realized**

"I-Operations creates"

BENEFIT — **Sustainable Impact in the Internet Economy**

INTERNET ECONOMY

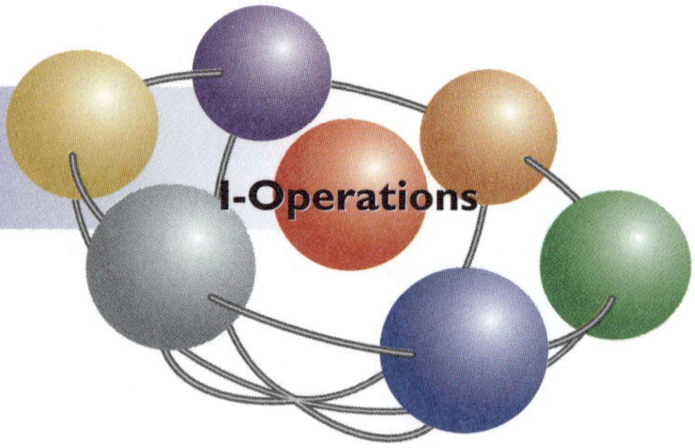

Appendix

Explanation of Research Approach

It is widely accepted by most observers that we are in a time of unprecedented change, and that the Internet is the catalyst for much of this change. Despite this mass of opinion, the task of measuring the impact of the Internet is elusive. While there have been attempts to quantify the Internet Economy, studies have typically focused on revenue generation, job creation or, in some cases, customer acquisition or market potential. These are indeed worthwhile efforts, but they leave unanswered the question: "How should end-to-end operations be transformed by Internet technologies?" This book tackles this topic.

The Internet has enabled individuals and companies to be more connected than ever before. The flow of information has accelerated at a staggering rate, and business is now done on Internet time. These factors have affected the definition of transactions, their speed, and the underlying operations of organizations. Our research, therefore, focuses on identifying the Internet-related drivers of change, and determining how they should influence the Operating Models of organizations. We want to know how successful companies in the Internet Economy function and what they did to become successful. Our objective is to distill the key characteristics and behaviors that enable a company to implement an Internet-enabled Operating Model.

As you should expect, our research is based on a statistically representative random sample of businesses. Some of the sampling questions with tabled results are provided in this Appendix.

We use a hybrid approach, consisting of both quantitative and qualitative research, for the following reasons:

- Broad-based quantitative research, while statistically valid, does not reach the group that has a cohesive view of their entire organization, namely, CxO-level executives.
- Past research did not cover all aspects of operations as an integrated whole, but focused on areas that were thought to be most interesting. We therefore use proprietary tools that enable us to take a 360-degree look at an organization. We can then identify all domains that are impacted by the Internet.
- We need an inside look at those companies that we believe exhibit a functioning Internet-enabled Operating Model. What do they do differently? We have, therefore, developed a spreading CxO-referral approach. Executives who are interviewed lead us to those whom they consider to be the best in the business.
- We want to investigate a range of corporations employing varying degrees of Internet technology. In addition to the e-business leaders, we therefore specifically target organizations that might be grappling with the implementation of an Internet-enabled Operating Model within a traditional business environment.
- We corroborate the quantitative research, and explore certain areas in more depth in the qualitative phase.
- A final reason we choose to use blended research lies in the nature of the topic. The Internet has created a business environment that is constantly evolving. One of the weaknesses of quantitative research is that it only gives the researcher a snapshot of the current state. That is, a project

based solely on quantitative research would be effective in explaining and describing only the current situation.

By using a mix of both quantitative and qualitative research, we are able to get a more comprehensive view of the situation facing companies today, as well as valuable insights into what we will see in the future. Our goal, however, is to be forward-looking. We want to know where the Internet Economy is going, and what the implications will be for end-to-end operations. Interviews and observations provide us with a deeper understanding of the underlying issues concerning the impact of the Internet within specific companies.

Conclusion

Significant work was performed by our team, with the support of Cisco Systems and The Institute for Innovation, Integration & Impact. We are satisfied that the results obtained are valid, informative and at the same time, forward-looking. We used statistically valid populations and sample sizes, and analyzed the results in a manner consistent with acceptable research practices.

We trust that these insights into I-Operations will be useful to a wide variety of organizations.

I-Operations Baseline Survey 2000

The I-Operations Baseline survey was executed in two phases.

The first was a quantitative survey that included over 500 respondents from companies with greater than 100 employees. The Dun & Bradstreet Office Intensive File served as the frame from which the sample was selected. This file is a subset of the entire Dun & Bradstreet (D&B) Database and includes over three million firms that meet the D&B criteria for increased likelihood to buy office products. These criteria are based on industry (SIC), size (revenue and number of employees), and sit type (headquarters, branch or subsidiary).

The second phase was a qualitative phase conducted with high-level executives. We used a question set as our discussion guide for the interviews, and the results of the question set follows. As mentioned in the previous section, "Explanation of Research," we used a 0 to 5 scale:

0 = Not Applicable
1 = Strongly Disagree
2 = Disagree
3 = Neutral
4 = Agree
5 = Strongly Agree

A sub-set of statements that were used in our interviews follows. The questions listed correspond to the survey results displayed in our tables throughout the book. They by no means represent the entirety of our research.

Explanation of research diagrams

Our research is displayed in tables throughout the book using dials to represent the survey results. Our respondents were asked to rank the statements using a scale of 0 to 5.

0 = No basis for providing an answer or response
1 = Strongly Disagree
2 = Disagree
3 = Neutral
4 = Agree
5 = Strongly Agree

The dials show the average of the results, where 1 is on the left and 5 is on the right. For example, the dial below is representative of an average response of 4.20 (somewhere between "Agree" and "Strongly Agree"). In most of the tables we show only the results of companies we have determined to be leaders in the new economy, and in others we show the results of the average from the entire group of respondents. In each case we are careful to explain which set of results we are displaying.

Statement	Survey Results
Internet-based technologies make it easier to identify, build and leverage an ecosystem of partners.	

Statement	Survey Results
Lack of vision is a significant hindrance to developing I-Operations.	4.60
Lack of knowledge of Internet technologies is a significant hindrance to investing in the Internet.	5.00
The greatest inhibitor of product innovation is legacy systems.	2.67
The greatest inhibitor of product innovation is legacy people—old thinking.	4.50
The greatest inhibitor of product innovation is the absence of a clear, repeatable, predictable product development approach.	4.33
We enable customers to see deeper into the back end operations of the company via Internet technologies.	4.25
The Internet enables operating models to be more customer-facing.	4.60
The boundaries between front and back end systems are being deliberately erased.	4.83
Internet-based technologies make it easier to identify, build and leverage an ecosystem of partners.	4.20
Who has access to company information via Internet-enabled technologies?	
Customers	5.00
Employees	5.00
Suppliers/Partners	4.20
Distributors/Vendors	5.00
Investors	4.83
Internet-enabled Applications have enabled us to more efficiently interact with:	
Customers	5.00
Suppliers	4.50
Distributors	5.00
The Media	4.75
Partners	4.75
Investors	4.67
We recognize that Internet Strategy is really business strategy.	5.00
Internet-based communications have improved our interaction with customers.	5.00
Internet browsers are becoming the most utilized interface within our organization.	5.00
Internet browser applications will be the common link between all parties of interest.	4.67

Statement	Survey Results
Using Internet/network based technologies customers can:	
Look up corporate information	5.00
Look up product information	5.00
Buy products	5.00
Check account status	5.00
Personalize website	5.00
The lack of integration between our own front end and back end office systems is a challenge to our e-business.	1.33
Company information should be accessible via the Web in order to help employees manage clients, customers, suppliers and distributors.	5.00
Senior executives are more in touch with constituents using Internet technologies.	4.33
Internet-based communications have enabled clearer lines of communication between divisions of the company.	5.00
Employees have the ability to easily communicate with executives.	4.80
Internet-based technologies enable us to remove process inefficiencies at the borders between corporations.	4.00
We leverage Internet technologies to manage partners.	4.20
Internet-based communications allow more people to be involved in decision-making in our organization.	4.50
Decision-making is more democratic as a result of implementing Internet technologies.	3.33
Decision-making takes place where it is most appropriate (due to more relevant, timely and free flowing information).	4.00

Glossary of Terms

Application. The term application is a shorter form of application program. An application program is a program designed to perform a specific function directly for the user or, in some cases, for another application program.

Application Service Provider. ASP—An organization that hosts software applications on its own servers within its own facilities. Customers access the application via private lines or the Internet. Also called a "commercial service provider."

B2B. Business-to-Business—business transactions conducted between two or more businesses using the Internet as the primary vehicle for the transactions.

B2C. Business-to-Consumer—business transactions conducted between a business and multiple end consumers using the Internet as the primary vehicle for the transactions.

Back end. Systems that are used to support business processes historically not visible to the end customer.

Brick and Mortar. A traditional organization whose assets and service delivery mechanisms are primarily physical.

C 'e2e' O. Chief end-to-end Officer. Someone who is responsible for overseeing the integration of the Internet into the end-to-end operations of a corporation.

Clicks and Mortar. Also called "bricks and clicks," refers to businesses that offer online services via the Web as well as the more traditional bricks and mortar business. Coined in 1999 by David Pottruck, co-CEO of the Charles Schwab brokerage firm, when referring to the integration of the online e-Schwab business with the traditional Charles Schwab brokerage business.

Converged Networks. The delivery of voice, data and video over the same (IP) networks.

Customer Facing. Business processes that are readily visible to end customers, such as ordering and customer service. Also known as Front End.

e-Business. Electronic-Business—Doing business online. The term is often used synonymously with e-commerce, but e-business is more of an umbrella term for having a broad business on the Web. An e-business site may be very comprehensive and offer more than just selling its products and services. For example, it may feature a general search facility or the ability to track shipments or have threaded discussions.

e-Commerce. Electronic Commerce—Doing business online, typically via the Web. It is also called "e-business," "e-tailing" and "I-commerce." Although in most cases e-commerce and e-business are synonymous, e-commerce implies that goods and services can be purchased online, whereas e-business might be used as more of an umbrella term for a total presence on the Web, which would naturally include the e-commerce (shopping) component.

Ecosystem. A network of organizations/companies that work together to achieve a common purpose. See Impact Network.

EDI. Electronic Data Interchange—EDI pre-dates the Internet, and includes the electronic communication of business transactions, such as orders, confirmations and invoices, between organizations. Third parties provide EDI services that enable organizations with different equipment to connect. Although interactive access may be a part of it, EDI implies direct computer-to-computer transactions into vendors' databases and ordering systems. On the technical side, the Internet is expected to give EDI quite a boost, but not by using private networks and the traditional EDI data formats. Rather, XML is expected to be the glue that connects businesses together using the Web as the communications vehicle.

e-Learning. Using the Internet as a medium for education; also referred to as distance learning, and webucation.

Employee empowerment. Applications and policies that enable employees of a corporation to have self-service access to their company's employee services and benefits.

e-Support. Customer self-service applications utilizing Internet capabilities.

External stakeholders. Individuals or organizations that are outside of the corporation and have a stake in its success or failure. These include but are not limited to customers, shareholders, boards, distributors, suppliers and partners.

Front end. Business processes that are readily visible to end customers, such as ordering and customer service. Also known as Customer Facing.

Horizontal Business Application. An application that enables or carries out a set of business processes that are common to many industries and/or functions within organizations.

The I^4 Methodology™. The Institute's proprietary intellectual framework for assisting leaders in defining impact, and working through the innovations, investments and integration (corporate alignment) needed to maximize such impact. Comprises numerous tools that greatly increase the speed of developing corporate strategy and enabling implementation.

I.T. Information Technology.

Impact. The end result that a corporation wants to achieve, often measured in terms of the desired effect on customers, clients or target audience of the corporation. It may also extend to the other stakeholders such as shareholders, employees, business partners and the community.

Impact Assessment™. A corporate X-Ray that measures Desired Impact vs. Current, Competitor or Future Impact across all aspects of the Operating Model.

Impact Network™. The sub-set of customers, competitors, contributors (suppliers) and complementors that deliberately band together to create an impact.

Innovation. The deliberate and systematic consideration of applying fresh thinking to every aspect of a corporation's Operating Model, including the consideration of how trends can be leveraged to enhance impact.

Institute. The Institute for Innovation, Integration & Impact, Inc. A corporation whose objective is *Partnering with leaders to maximize Impact*™. The Institute goes beyond traditional strategy and management consulting companies, having *The Head of a Think Tank, the Hands of a Business, and the Heart of Philanthropy*™. The Institute spurs clients to dream about Impact with predictable Innovation, and helps to turn these dreams into reality. With Web-enabled diagnostic skills and comprehensive measurement tools, The Institute helps ensure corporate alignment, or Integration. See www.inst.net for more details.

Integrated Convergence Applications. Applications that have a holistic or integrated view of how the end user uses information, seeking to deliver such information and functionality across a spectrum of delivery mechanisms (such as PDA, cell phone, pocket computer, mobile IP phone, IP phone, and Web browser) in as seamless a manner as possible.

Integration. A state of collaboration between and alignment among all aspects of the Operating Model, toward the end of producing maximized impact.

Internal stakeholders. Those parties internal to a corporation who contribute to and benefit from the well being of the corporation.

Internet. The technologies comprising the deployment of all Internet, intranets, extranets and the World Wide Web, for all types of information including voice, video, data, and image.

Internet Economy. The new business context in which all corporations now operate, brought about mainly by the advent of the Internet. Also known as New World Economy.

Internet-enabled. The use of New World Applications in a virtual enterprise.

IP. Internetworking Protocol—A connectionless protocol that uses datagrams, or data packets, for sending data between networks.

Internet Revolution. The massive changes throughout society brought about by the Internet, comparable to the Industrial Revolution which was stimulated by the invention of the steam engine and breakthroughs in textile manufacturing technologies.

Internet Speed. The increased rate of change experienced by corporations participating in the Internet Economy.

Internet Time. See Internet Speed.

Invest. The deliberate consideration and required application of resources to all aspects of the Operating Model, not limited to capital, also inclusive of cultural change and people development in a way that readies them for having an impact.

I-Operations. Internet-enabled Operating Models.

Knowledge Worker. A professional who performs knowledge work. Often associated with the creation of intellectual capital in collaboration with others, thereby emphasizing the importance of technologies that support such collaboration.

Legacy Systems/Applications. An older and usually technologically obsolete computer system such as a mainframe or minicomputer, or an application that has been in existence for some time. In today's world of the Internet, virtually anything not Web related is often thought of as a legacy application or system.

Legacy thinking. The perception that migration from a legacy system to more current technologies will either be too expensive or will cause business disruptions or will not yield business benefits.

Net. Abbreviated form for Internet.

Net-enabled. See Internet-enabled.

New World Application. An application that ostensibly utilizes the Internet to significantly improve the profitability or market share of a company.

New World Economy. See Internet Economy.

Old World Economy. Pre-Internet Economy.

Operating Model. The processes and procedures an organization uses to design, build, market and manage its products and services.

Operations. The execution of the Operating Model.

P2P. Has various definitions depending on who is speaking: Peer to Peer, Portal to Portal, Person to Person.

Physical Enterprise. A business or organization comprised of people and assets with a common objective.

Pure Internet Play. A corporation whose business could not exist outside of the Internet. Also referred to as Pure Play.

Pure Play. See Pure Internet Play.

Virtual Development. The synergistic product design and development among multiple geographic locations enabled by the Internet.

Value Discipline. The focusing of a corporation's core competencies around a specific way of adding value to customers, namely, product leadership, operational excellence, or customer intimacy. The Old World Economy theory was that a corporation could only excel at one value discipline.

Virtual Close. The ability to close the books at any time. First pioneered by Cisco, and now a hallmark of companies that have the process efficiencies and agility associated with the Internet Economy.

Virtual Enterprise. An organizing principle for internal and external entities who share in information access, decision-making and value creation activities.

Virtual Manufacturing. The ability to manufacture products outside of a corporation's own boundaries and in a manner that is transparent to customers.

Voice over IP. Also called IP Telephony. VoIP is the two-way transmission of phone conversations over an IP network, allowing audio to travel over the Internet, intranets, or private LANs and WANs.

End Notes

1. *Tracking the Internet Economy: 100 Numbers you need to Know*, Booz-Allen Hamilton and The Economist, as taken from The Industry Standard Sept 13, 1999. www.thestandard.com/research/metrics/display/0,2799,9801,00.html
2. I-Operations Baseline Survey 2000
3. *The Internet Economy Indicators* (www.internetindicators.com)
4. *Tracking the Internet Economy: 100 Numbers you need to Know*, Forrester Research as taken from The Industry Standard Sept 13, 1999. www.thestandard.com/research/metrics/display/0,2799,9801,00.html
5. U.S. Department of Commerce
6. Figures provided by Cisco's investor relations group and are for Q1/FY01. In Q4 2002, Revenue per employee was down to $540,000, and headcount was around 35,500.
7. Figures provided by AutoNation Inc. Ft. Lauderdale, FL Used with Permission.
8. *Venture Capital Fundraising Doubles in the Second Quarter* www.nvca.org/VEpress08_21_00.html
9. *Revamping the Corporation From the Inside Out*, by Gary Hamel, Business 2.0 September 26, 2000 (136).
10. *The Dream Society*, by Rolf Jensen, Mcgraw Hill 1999.
11. *Turning an Economy Inside Out*, The Delphi Group, November 17, 1999 (12).
12. Cisco Systems' Investor Relations page. www.cisco.com
13. I-Operations Baseline Survey 2000
14. I-Operations Baseline Survey 2000
15. I-Operations Baseline Survey 2000
16. I-Operations Baseline Survey 2000 (qualitative)
17. *Boo.com: A Cautionary Tale*, by Susan Orenstein, May 29, 2000 www.thestandard.com/article/display/0,1151,15450,00.html
18. *Boo.com goes bust*, from TNL.net www.tnl.net/newsletter/2000/boobust.asp
19. *e or Be Eaten*, by Stewart Alsop, Fortune, November 8, 1999 (87).
20. Michael Dell as quoted in *Why Dell's Approach Works*, by Eric Lundquist, eWEEK www.zdnet.com/eweek/stories/general/0,11011,2625950,00.html
21. Scott McNealy as quoted in *The Odd Couple* by Brent Schneider, Fortune, May 1, 2000 (120).
22. Robert Rubin as quoted in *Rubin: New Economy hasn't repealed laws of Economics*, by Dennis Callaghan, eWEEK www.zdnet.com/eweek/stories/general/0,11011,2645423,00.html
23. *e-Business: A Practical Perspective*, The Delphi Group, January 7, 2000 (13).
24. *Who Moved My Cheese?,* by Spencer Johnson, M.D., Putnam Publishing Group Sept 1998.
25. *Buying Into the New Economy,* by Mark Heinzl, Wall Street Journal, July 25, 2000.
26. From Cisco's Q1/FY01 customer satisfaction survey results
27. Webvan IPO information available at: www.ipo.com/ipoinfo/profile.asp?p=IPO&c=0001092657&pg=2

28. Pete Mountanous quote from I-Operations Baseline Survey 2000 (qualitative interview)
29. Pete Mountanous quote from I-Operations Baseline Survey 2000 (qualitative interview)
30. *Big Business Meets the e-World,* Erin Brown, Fortune, November 8, 1999 (95).
31. *e or Be Eaten,* by Stewart Alsop, Fortune, November 8 (86-87).
32. Chris Yates quote from EA.com I-Operations Baseline Survey 2000 (qualitative interview).
33. *Collision Course,* by Scott Kirsner, Fast Company, January/February 2000 (132).
34. Pete Mountanous quote from I-Operations Baseline Survey 2000 (qualitative interview).
35. www.maf.org
36. *Millionaires and the Millennium: New Estimates of the Forthcoming Wealth Transfer and the Prospects for a Golden Age of Philanthropy*, John J. Havens and Paul G. Schervish, October 19, 1999.
37. www.gem-werc.org
38. *Leading through Change*, by Brett Johnson, Christian Management Report, October, 2002.
39. *Guide to Distance Learning Programs 2001* (Peterson's Guide to Distance Learning Programs, 5th Ed), 2000.
40. *Log on for learning,* by Chris Tucker, Spirit Magazine, September, 2000 (42). By 2000 there were over 800 U.S. colleges and universities offering distance courses for credit, to their own and other students, mostly via the Web (Simonson et al.,2000).
41. *No Significant Difference Phenomenon,* by Thomas L. Russell, North Carolina State University, Raleigh NC, 1999.
42. *Perspectives: Webucation,* by James W. Michaels, Forbes May 15, 2000.
43. The Holy Bible NIV, Matthew 9:17. Zondervan Bible Publishing, Grand Rapids Michigan, 1988.
44. The Holy Bible NIV, Luke 5:39. Zondervan Bible Publishing, Grand Rapids Michigan, 1988.
45. *The Global Competitiveness Report 2000* www.weforum.org
46. *Revamping the Corporation From the Inside Out,* by Gary Hamel, Business 2.0 September 26, 2000 (136).
47. Office of Business and Industrial Analysis based on BEA and Bureau of Labor Statistics Data (Source: U.S. Department of Commerce).
48. *What's So New About the New Economy?*, by Anya Schiffrin, The Industry Standard, October 30, 2000. www.thestandard.com/article/display/0,1151,19677,00.html
49. *Michael Dell Urges Broader Business Integration of the Internet*, Dell Press Release September 21, 2000.
50. *What's So New About the New Economy?*, by Anya Schiffrin, The Industry Standard, October 30, 2000.
51. *Why Dell's Approach Works*, by Eric Lundquist, eWeek, September 10, 2000 www.zdnet.com/eweek/stories/general/0,11011,2625950,00.html
52. *The Internet Economy Indicators*, University of Texas, June 2000. www.internetindicators.com
53. *Dell says Internet integration key to business success,* by Joe Wilcox CNET News.com September 21, 2000 (URL:http://news.cnet.com/news/0-1003-200-2830947.html)

54. *Monica Luechtefeld Makes the Net Click,* by Linda Tischler, Fast Company, November 2002, Issue 64, page 122
55. *Tracking the Internet Economy: 100 Numbers you need to Know,* International Data Corp., as taken from The Industry Standard September 13, 1999. www.thestandard.com/research/metrics/display/0,2799,9801,00.html; updated from www.inq7.net, February 15, 2002
56. Cisco Networking Academy Program www.cisco.com
57. *Do You have the Will to Lead?,* by Peter Koestenbaum, Fast Company, March 2000 (222).
58. *Do You have the Will to Lead?,* by Peter Koestenbaum, Fast Company, March 2000 (222).
59. *Do You have the Will to Lead?,* by Peter Koestenbaum, Fast Company, March 2000 (222).
60. *The Phsychological Underpinnings of the 10-Fs,* by Dr. Art Wouters www.convergencebook.com
61. *The New Gospel of Academia,* by Teresa Watanabe, Los Angeles Times, October 29, 2000.
62. In research project conducted by Dr. Blake Bowden of Cincinnati Children's Hospital Center, 527 children were studied to determine characteristics linked to good mental health and adjustment. Those who ate meals with their families – whether at home or not – were least likely to take drugs, get depressed, or land in trouble with authorities.
63. *Leadership is an Art,* by Max Depree, Dell publishing 1989.
64. An example is Cisco's involvement in *Netaid.org*, and Hewlett Packard's *e-inclusion*.
65. *Convergence*, by Brett Johnson, The Institute Press 2000 (16-27).
66. *The Dream Society*, by Rolf Jensen, Mcgraw Hill 1999.
67. *The Dream Society*, by Rolf Jensen, Mcgraw Hill 1999.
68. *The Phsychological Underpinnings of the 10-Fs* by Dr. Art Wouters. www.convergencebook.com
69. The Holy Bible NIV, Psalm 78:72. Zondervan Bible Publishing, Grand Rapids Michigan, 1988.

Index